Light *the* Flame

ALSO BY ANDREW HARVEY

*The Hope: A Guide to Sacred Activism**

Radical Passion: Sacred Love and Wisdom in Action

The Way of Passion: A Celebration of Rumi

*Available from Hay House
Please visit:

Hay House USA: **www.hayhouse.com®**
Hay House Australia: **www.hayhouse.com.au**
Hay House UK: **www.hayhouse.co.uk**
Hay House South Africa: **www.hayhouse.co.za**
Hay House India: **www.hayhouse.co.in**

ॐ

Light *the* Flame

365 Days of Prayer

Andrew Harvey

HAY HOUSE, INC.
Carlsbad, California • New York City
London • Sydney • Johannesburg
Vancouver • Hong Kong • New Delhi

Published and distributed in the United States by: Hay House, Inc.:
www.hayhouse.com® • *Published and distributed in Australia by:*
Hay House Australia Pty. Ltd.: www.hayhouse.com.au • *Published
and distributed in the United Kingdom by:* Hay House UK, Ltd.:
www.hayhouse.co.uk • *Published and distributed in the Republic
of South Africa by:* Hay House SA (Pty), Ltd.: www.hayhouse.co.za
• *Distributed in Canada by:* Raincoast: www.raincoast.com • *Published in India by:* Hay House Publishers India: www.hayhouse.co.in

Cover design: Karla Baker • *Interior design:* Nick C. Welch

Library of Congress Cataloging-in-Publication Data

Light the flame : 365 days of prayer / [compiled by] Andrew Harvey.
    pages cm
ISBN 978-1-4019-4313-4 (pbk.)
1. Prayers. I. Harvey, Andrew, 1952-, editor of compilation.
BL560L495 2013
204'.33--dc23
                                        2013011419

Tradepaper ISBN: 978-1-4019-4313-4

16 15 14 13   4 3 2 1
1st edition, November 2013

Printed in the United States of America

SUSTAINABLE
FORESTRY
INITIATIVE
Certified Chain of Custody
Promoting Sustainable Forestry
www.sfiprogram.org
SFI-01268

SFI label applies to the cover stock

Nancy Walker Koppelman
Beloved Friend

From joy all beings come, in joy all
Beings live, to joy all beings return.

—TAITTIRIYA UPANISHAD

CONTENTS

FOREWORD

With this book, Andrew Harvey has provided a long-awaited and much-needed gift—a book of prayers. People need to pray and many, surprisingly, do not know how. Aside from petition or emergency prayers, they have no experience of the bliss that one finds in the daily practice of reflecting upon illuminated words that draw you inward, away from the distractions of ordinary life.

Prayer is power. That is a simple way to define the nature of prayer. I came to appreciate the power of prayer during the time that I wrote *Entering the Castle,* a book about the mystical teachings of St. Teresa of Ávila. I had always considered myself to be someone who lived a prayerful life, but it wasn't until I delved into the writings of this great saint that I grappled with what it meant to withdraw from one state of consciousness in order to enter into a much deeper place of silence. Teresa described this place as one's "interior castle"—her metaphor for the soul. She said that entry into your soul requires prayer. Your mind is an insufficient instrument when it comes to gaining access to the higher planes of consciousness. You must "pray your way in."

I found her guidance intriguing, and so I followed it. Day after day I concentrated on praying, at first with great mental determination—not petition prayer, but devotional. I followed a practice of hers in which I reflected upon a mystical teaching and waited for something to happen. *Like what?* you may wonder. I guess I was waiting for what she described as an experience of "quietude." In other words, I was trying to force a mystical experience. Finally, I gave up and just maintained a prayer practice.

After a few months, I noticed that something had shifted in me. It wasn't a dramatic shift, as if I'd had an epiphany and suddenly knew my life needed to go in a different direction. Rather, the changes I felt were deeply and richly internal, subtle in their expression in keeping with the delicate nature of grace. I noticed, for example, that I had a sense of calm pulsating inside of me that was slightly contrary to my high-strung nature. It felt divine in some oddly organic way. That feeling has never left me, and I have never stopped my prayer practice.

Once someone asked me, "Do you have any prayers that work?"

"Prayers that work?" I responded. I knew what she meant, of course. Did I have any magical prayers she could recite that would result in her getting what she wanted in three days—like those chain e-mails that assure people that good things will happen to them in 24 hours if they forward the message to 20 other people. I've had count-less conversations with people reporting to me that they "pray and pray and nothing ever changes," suggesting that prayer is the culprit.

"Why should I pray?" another person recently asked.

"Your alternative strikes me as leading you into hope-lessness, but it's your choice," I said.

Ultimately, the choice to take five minutes a day to withdraw from chaos and distraction and enter into the quietness of your inner self is yours alone. If you do so choose, then imagine you are retreating into your "interior castle," your private sanctuary for a silent moment with the Divine, and trust in the truth that you are, at your core, holy.

Thank you, Andrew Harvey. You have given us all a treasure trove of blessings with this book.

Caroline Myss
Oak Park

INTRODUCTION

In prayer, we open the whole of our being to God; we go beyond all the limited processes of the rational mind and open ourselves to the One to which all words and thoughts are pointing. This is not easy, but through deep devotion and self-surrender over time, we uncover the mystery of a nondual, infinitely loving relationship with the Divine that initiates us into what Jesus called "the peace beyond understanding."

Light the Flame has been designed specifically for our time in three ways. First, it draws on the wisdom and truth of all of the mystical traditions. We are witnessing the birth of a universal mysticism, in which all of the different ways of loving God and the creation are celebrated. In my life, I have had the grace and privilege of being initiated into many of these mystical traditions. This has given my prayer life a multifaceted and exhilarating wealth of richness and emotion. I want to share this wealth with you, so that in whatever tradition you find yourself, you can also be inspired by the joy and wisdom of other great visions of the Divine.

Second, the prayers in *Light the Flame* are short. This is for two reasons: I myself have found that repeating shorter prayers has an enormous power to open a door between the human and the Divine. I also know we are all under tremendous pressure; we live in a world addicted to hurry and distraction. Using short prayers devotedly and repeatedly over the course of our harried days is a practical way to keep the compass of our being turned to the true north of the Beloved.

Third, the world is in crisis, which demands of us both an unprecedented allegiance to inner transformation and a commitment to sacredly inspired action. We must truly ground our lives in the divine presence, however we understand it.

The prayers I have selected are geared to help us dive deeply into our divine nature, so as to meet the challenges of this time with faith, grace, and generosity of soul.

Prayer has saved my life. Without it, I should have been a lunatic long ago. I had my share of the bitterest public and private experiences. They threw me in temporary despair. If I was able to get rid of that despair, it was because of prayer.

—MAHATMA GANDHI

That prayer has great power, which a human being makes with all his or her might. It makes a sour heart sweet, a sad heart joyful, a poor heart rich, a fooling heart wise, a shrinking heart brave, a sick heart well, a blind heart full of sight, a frozen heart ardent.
It draws down the great God into the tiny heart. It drives the famished soul up into the fullness of God. It brings together two lovers, God and the soul, in a sublime place where they speak long of love.

—MECHTHILD OF MAGDEBURG

The Great Spirit is everywhere. The Great Spirit hears whatever is in our minds and hearts and it is not necessary to speak to Him in a loud voice.

—BLACK ELK

O Lord, give me a heart
I can pour out in thanksgiving,
Give me life
So I can spend it
Working for the salvation of the world.

—SHEIKH ANSARI

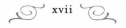

JANUARY

JANUARY 1

Lead me into that holy drunkenness,
The domain of the uncontrollable,
Of the divine power that breaks all bounds,
That breaks down all barriers, that fills me
To the last cells of my body, with the Holy Spirit.

—ANDREW HARVEY

January 2

O love, O pure deep love,
Be here, be now, be all.
Worlds dissolve into your stainless radiance,
Frail living leaves burn with you
Brighter than cold stars:
Make me your servant, your breath, your core.

—Rumi

January 3

However innumerable sentient beings are,
I vow to save them.
However inexhaustible the defilements are,
I vow to extinguish them.
However immeasurable the *dharmas* are,
I vow to master them.
However incomparable enlightenment is,
I vow to attain it.

—Bodhisattva vows

January 4

O God,
a child is crying,
shivering,
abandoned in the dark of nights poverty and war.
He is from the land of Africa.
She is from Palestine, Syria or Thailand.
She is a Jew from Jerusalem
or a Christian born in the ghettoes of Chicago.
Her tears have broken your heart, O beloved Divine.
You woke us up and called us to act.
May we heed your call.
May our hearts become mighty
and our spirits inconsolable,
until that child and all her sisters and brothers
are unfolded in our humanity,
and held in the love we speak of so often,
and pray for.
May our love of justice
be the compassion that guides us,
and the passion
that steers our path.
May we take that child into our arms
and remember that whatever is her color,
her race or creed,
she is our own.
She is the children of the world,
the trust you laid in our hands.

—Chris Saade

JANUARY 5

Let us meditate
On the Glorious Splendor
Of the Divine Light.
May it illuminate our meditation.

—THE GAYATRI MANTRA

JANUARY 6

Blessed are those who await in tears
The great dawn of Liberation,
Fruit of Divine grace and human struggle:
Your eyes will see the glory
Of the sun's rays of justice.

—LEONARDO BOFF

JANUARY 7

O noblest greening
Who have your roots in the sun
Green the depths of my being.

—HILDEGARD OF BINGEN

January 8

To look inhumanity in the face, Lord,
Is to know its madness can take hold of me.
May I never forget this, Lord, in false hope
Or a too-great reliance on my shaky powers.
May I have the courage, dignity, peace, and passion,
In spite of everything in me and the world,
To stay human.

—Andrew Harvey, inspired by Etty Hillesum

JANUARY 9

For as long as space exists
And sentient beings endure,
May I too remain
To dispel the misery of the world.

—SHANTIDEVA

January 10

Give Me Light

O God, give me light in my heart and light in my tongue
and light in my hearing and light in my seeing and light
in my feelings and light in every part of my body and light
before me and light behind me. Give me, I beg you,
light on my right hand and light on my left hand and light
above me and light beneath me. O Lord, make light grow
within me and give me light and illuminate me.

—The Prophet Muhammad

JANUARY 11

Prayer for Tolerance

O Thou God of all beings, of all worlds and of all times
We pray that the little differences in our clothes
in our inadequate languages
in our ridiculous customs
in our imperfect laws
in our illogical opinions
in our ranks and conditions, which
are so exaggeratedly important to us
and so meaningless to you,
that these small variations
that distinguish those atoms that we call human beings
one from another,
may not be signals of hatred and persecution.

—VOLTAIRE

January 12

O my soul, I have given you everything
Even my last possession
All my hands are now empty.

That I should pray you to sing
Is my last thing to give! So sing, my soul, sing
A song of the highest mountains, of the New Human!
Even if I die, I will listen.

—Friedrich Nietzsche

JANUARY 13

Star of this stormy sea . . .
Turn your heart to the terrifying squall
In which I find myself,
Alone,
Without a map.

—PETRARCH

January 14

May my mind become firm
Like a rock
And no longer shake
In this world
Where everything is shadows.

—The Buddha

January 15

Strengthen us, O God, to relieve the oppressed, to hear the groans of poor prisoners, to reform the abuses of all professions; that many be made not poor to make a few rich; for Jesus Christ's sake.

—Oliver Cromwell

January 16

With the whole earth as my altar, may I, Lord, offer up
To you incessantly, the travails and agonies of the world.

—Andrew Harvey, inspired by Teilhard de Chardin

January 17

Give me, O Lord, the courage I need
In good and bad and perseverance too
Rekindle all my hope and faith in You
And burn from my heart every vain desire.

—Mary, Queen of Scots

January 18

Let me accept the defeats that have adorned my journey.

Let me learn that for the freedom of my Spirit
and for the liberation of the broken ones,
I can endure the struggle to love and offer my passion
as a sweet and sacred offering to you O God.

Let me kneel when others pray with their tears
and stand fierce for justice when children are exiled
to a dark plight.

The road is long
and the storms are raging
and sometimes weariness
overcomes me.
Yet let the flame of love
reawaken me
to the eternal.
The eternal that will never subside
The eternal that is present
in every aspiration
for solidarity
and in every yearning
for a love that is unbounded,
like your love, O God everlasting,
O lover of our spirits and our world.

—CHRIS SAADE

JANUARY 19

Homage to You, Tara,
Whose fingers adorn Your Heart
With the sublime gemstone
Of the three precious jewels.

May your wheel of mind energy
Whirl in my direction
The dazzling radiance of Your innate light.

—BUDDHIST PRAYER

January 20

O my God, may I always adore You as the life of all things. You are the life of plants and birds, of animals and fields and forests, of the great snow-peaked mountains adamant in Your eternal silence. The depth of Your immense life pours out on every living thing. May I become conscious of that immense life and live, at all moments, to praise and glorify Thy name.

—Jean-Jacques Olier

January 21

Christ, you have revealed to me that the
Ever-new magical universe is continually
Reborn in the child and that only the grown-up
Was banished from Eden. You have shown me that
It is the child that eats of the Tree of Life and
That for him the Laws of the Universe are
Magical. This childhood and this magic,
O Christ, Restore.

—ANDREW HARVEY, INSPIRED BY LEWIS THOMPSON

January 22

Prayer to Be Simple

My God, so gently life begins again today,
as yesterday and so many times before.
Like these butterflies, like these laborers,
like these sun-devouring cicadas
and these blackbirds hidden in the cold dark leaves,
let me, oh my God, continue to live my life
as simply as possible.

—Francis Jammes

January 23

All my splendor is to burn in you
May I know this fire now devouring me
Is devouring itself ecstatically:
May I become this fire, dancing on my own bones.

—RUMI

JANUARY 24

May I always be a lamp unto myself.
May I always rely only on myself.
May I hold fast to the truth as to a lamp.
May I always see liberation in truth alone.

—HIMALAYAN BUDDHIST PRAYER

January 25

Steadiness is essential.
Forwards or backwards
Let us not look.
Let us learn to live swaying
As a rocking boat on the sea.

—Friedrich Hölderlin

JANUARY 26

May I embody the nobility of Heaven
May I embody the humility of Earth
May I so unify in myself
The sacred attributes of Heaven and Earth
That I extend to eternity with them.

—LIU I-MING

January 27

O holy Virgin,
When you said Yes
To housing God in your womb
You asked, as its price,
For peace in the world
Redemption for all the lost
Eternal life for the dead.
May I always pray with you
That your sublime prayer be granted.

—Saint Peter Chrysologus

JANUARY 28

Mother Of Us All,
Facing the exploding horrors of our time
I want to go numb, and even sometimes to die
Teach me to keep my heart open in Hell.
Teach me to believe in the grace
Of your birthing mystery
That, even in deepest chaos and destruction,
Is forming the embryo of a new humanity.

—ANDREW HARVEY

January 29

Holy Prajnaparamita
Mother-wisdom of emptiness,
Birth-cradle of all the Buddhas,
Release me from all deadly concepts of Separation,
Heal my longings for private liberation
In this life and all others
So I can live in the splendor of the Bodhisattva Vow
And go on dedicating all I am and do
To the liberation of all sentient beings everywhere.

—TIBETAN PRAYER

JANUARY 30

May I constrain all things to flow to me and into me
So from my endless fountain can gush free gifts of love.

—FRIEDRICH NIETZSCHE

January 31

God take my will and my life, and guide me how to live.

—Adapted from Step 3 in the Narcotics Anonymous
12-step program

FEBRUARY

FEBRUARY 1

Give me ecstasy, give me naked wonder, O my Creator!
Give birth to the Beloved in me, and let this lover die.
Let a thousand wrangling desires become one Love.

—RUMI

FEBRUARY 2

May confusion dawn as wisdom.

—TIBETAN PRAYER

FEBRUARY 3

Lord Jesus Christ,
Son of God,
Have mercy on me.

—THE JESUS PRAYER

February 4

May the burning and tender
Power
Of your love
I beg you, Lord,
Ravish my soul
From all earthly things
So that I may die
For the love of my love.

—Saint Francis of Assisi

FEBRUARY 5

The Beloved has no body on earth but mine.
The Beloved has no hands on earth but mine.
Mine are the eyes through which the Beloved
Streams compassion to the world.
Mine are the hands with which the Beloved
Is to bless all beings.
May I have the grace to know this mystery,
The courage to give myself to it entirely,
And the strength to enact its truth in the world.

—ANDREW HARVEY, INSPIRED BY TERESA OF ÁVILA

February 6

May I be happy.
May I be peaceful.
May I be free.
May my friends be happy.
May my friends be peaceful.
May my friends be free.
May my enemies be happy.
May my enemies be peaceful.
May my enemies be free.
May all beings be happy.
May all beings be peaceful.
May all beings be free.

—Buddhist prayer

February 7

O mother, dance around your true devotees!
Dance yourself and make them dance wildly!
O mother, dance in the fire-lotus of my heart!
Dance, you ever-holy force of Brahman!
Dance in all your world-enslaving beauty!

—Sri Ramakrishna

FEBRUARY 8

Let me be silent
Let me be still.
I offer You the sound in my Heart
I offer You the breath in my Lungs
I offer You the tranquillity in my Soul.
Let me be silent
Let me be still
Hover over me. Amen.

—CAROLINE MYSS

FEBRUARY 9

May I find the real, and give it endlessly away.
May I grow rich and fling gold to all who ask.
May I live at the empty radiant heart of Paradox
And dance there always with you, cheek to cheek.

—RUMI

FEBRUARY 10

May that day come soon, Lord,
When after mastering space,
The winds, the tides, and gravitation,
We harness for you the energies of love.
For on that day, Lord,
For the second time
In the history of the world,
We shall discover fire.

—ANDREW HARVEY, INSPIRED BY TEILHARD DE CHARDIN

FEBRUARY 11

Do what pleases You. I desire it.
Destroy me, I am happy.
Annihilate me, it is my will.
Rend me in pieces, break and burn me—
Let everything be to Your desire.
I am Yours and belong wholly to You.

—MADAME CHANTAL

February 12

David's Song of Praise

Give thanks to the Lord,
call on his name;
make his deeds known
to all people!
Sing to God, sing praises to him;
dwell on all his wondrous works!
Give praise to God's holy name!
Let the hearts rejoice
of all those seeking the Lord!
Pursue the Lord and his strength;
seek his face always!

—1 Chronicles 16:8–11

February 13

O Lord, love me intensely, love me long.
The more often You love me, the purer I shall be:
The more passionately You love me,
The more beautiful I will become.
The longer and deeper You love me,
The holier I shall be here on earth.

—Mechthild of Magdeburg

FEBRUARY 14

On this holy night
With sweet dew falling
On all the world
May my soul walk in your courtyard
Wholly exposed
Prepared for the mystical birth.

On this night of tender love
May we meet wholly
And I see coming into being before me
Our Divine child.

—SAINT GERTRUDE OF HELFTA

FEBRUARY 15

Lord
Let your mystery dawn in me
As an ecstasy of humility.

—SUFI PRAYER

FEBRUARY 16

May my prayer
Be pure and unstained
So this holy breath
That pours from my lips
Can join with the breath of Heaven
That is always flowing
Into me from above
So the spark of God within me
Is reunited with the Fire.

—HASIDIC PRAYER

FEBRUARY 17

O Black Madonna,
glorious dark one,
do what is necessary
to wake us up,
and give us
the strength and sacred passion
to bear our illumination.

—ANDREW HARVEY

February 18

Remind us O God,
of your dream for a planet that upholds love.

Remind us O God,
of your dream for a planet that evolves the
consciousness of peace, freedom,
justice, solidarity, compassion and inclusion.

Remind us O God,
of your dream for our Earth.

Remind us O God,
that you are forging a consciousness
that can manifest the splendour of your love.

Remind us O God,
that this Earth is to be the abode of peace, of freedom,
of justice, of solidarity,
of compassion and inclusion.

Remind us O God,
that we are the co-creators of your dream.

Remind us O God,
that we were born from love and for love
and that we are never to cease our work until this Earth
reflects the majesty
of your love.

—Chris Saade

FEBRUARY 19

O God give me strength
To be victorious over myself,
So nothing may chain me to this life.
O guide my spirit, raise me from these dark depths
So my soul, transformed by Your wisdom
May fearlessly strive upwards in fiery flight
For You alone understand and can inspire me.

—LUDWIG VAN BEETHOVEN

FEBRUARY 20

May I be a shadow
Far from dark villages
And drink God's silence
Out of the deep wells of the trees

—GEORG TRAKL

FEBRUARY 21

O God to those who have hunger
Give bread
And to us who have bread
Give hunger for justice.

—LATIN-AMERICAN PRAYER

FEBRUARY 22

O God, I praise You for the universe which You have evolved over unending centuries, vitalizing matter with energy, bringing forth all things as the peak of Your creating wisdom, working to unify mankind, initiating a process of spiritualizing humanity. O Creator God, let me be a willing partner in building the universe of Your will and in divinizing humanity, in unity with You permeating Your creation with love and incorporating souls into the eternal.

—TEILHARD DE CHARDIN

FEBRUARY 23

Lord, may we love all Your creation—
All the earth and every grain of sand in it.
May we love every leaf, every ray of Your light.
For we acknowledge to You that all life is
Like an ocean, all is flowing and blending
And that to withhold any measure of
Love from anything in Your universe
Is to withhold the same measure from You.

—FYODOR DOSTOYEVSKY

FEBRUARY 24

O Mother, take thy virtue, take thy vice,
And give me pure love for thee.
Here, take thy ignorance, take thy knowledge
Give me only pure love for thee.

—SRI RAMAKRISHNA

FEBRUARY 25

May I, more than all else,
Cherish at heart that love
That makes me live
A limitless life in this world.

—KABIR

February 26

Everything is close against my face
Everything close to my face is stone.

I am in anguish and have so little knowledge
Break in, Lord,
So your great transformation will happen to me
And my great grief-cry will happen to You.

—Andrew Harvey, inspired by Rainer Maria Rilke

February 27

I Abandon Myself to You

My Father, I abandon myself to you.
Do with me as You will.
Whatever you may do with me, I thank you.
I am prepared for anything; I accept everything.
Provided your will is fulfilled in me and in all creatures
I ask for nothing more, my God.
I place my soul in your hands.
I give it to you, my God,
With all the love of my heart
Because I love you.
And for me it is a necessity of love,
This gift of myself,
This placing of myself in your hands
Without reserve
In boundless confidence
Because you are my Father.

—Charles de Foucauld

FEBRUARY 28

May I be one of those
Who strive ceaselessly
For perfect enlightenment
And realize that emptiness
Whose essence is boundless compassion

—NAGARJUNA

FEBRUARY 29

May we become the longing of our ancestors and the
prayers of the forgotten children
May we hear the howling of animals, those abused and
those being annihilated
May our courage be an offering to you O God
And may our compassion become the fire of our hearts
May we respond to the pain of our world
May we kneel and prostrate to the vision of the heart
May we love without limit
Love until we discover in us the divine force
Love until we come to know our true names
And act for justice, for solidarity, for democratic freedoms,
animal rights and the protection of the earth
Act as One
United in our passion to serve
O God to strive for your dream of peace
and a thriving planet
and the end of all violence, economic, racial and that of
the sword

—CHRIS SAADE

MARCH

MARCH 1

Lord, make me humbler every hour
For humility alone can scoop away
The barren sand of my self-conceit
So my fountain may rest solidly upon the Rock.

—GENERAL CHARLES GEORGE GORDON

MARCH 2

I want no physical beauty
Or wealth or fame
Give me only illumination of the soul!

—SRI RAMAKRISHNA

March 3

O great God
You who see and uphold everything
I pray to You
That I find what I seek!
Yet let Your will be done!

—Andrew Harvey, inspired by a Sioux Indian prayer

MARCH 4

And no one knows . . .
But meanwhile, let me walk
And pick wild berries
To quench the love I have for you
Upon your paths, O earth.

—FRIEDRICH HÖLDERLIN

MARCH 5

Help Me, Lord

Lashed by desire
I roamed the streets of Good and Evil.
What did I gain? Nothing—
The fire of desire grew only fiercer:
As long as life goes on breathing in me
Help me, Lord—
You alone hear my prayer.

—SHEIKH ANSARI

MARCH 6

Between me and You, there is only me.
Take away the me, so only You remain.

—MANSUR AL-HALLAJ

MARCH 7

Whatever horrors men lead me through, for love's sake
I pray to stand firm and not be wounded by them
For I understand from the nobility of my soul
That in suffering for sublime love, I conquer.

—HADEWIJCH OF ANTWERP

March 8

Camel, Lion, Child

Let my spirit become a camel
And walk with its dark load into the wilderness;
And, in the wilderness, let it become a lion
Wrestling down and killing the dragon of false morality.
Then, O miracle, let the lion become the child
A dancing innocence and a holy Yes.

—Friedrich Nietzsche

MARCH 9

O Lord, grant us to love Thee:
Grant that we may love those that love Thee;
Grant that we may do the deeds that win Thy love.

—THE PROPHET MUHAMMAD

MARCH 10

This is what I want to happen, that our earth mother
May be clothed in ground corn four times over,
That frost flowers cover her over entirely,
That the mountain pines far away over there
May stand close to each other in the cold,
That the weight of snow crack some branches!
In order that the country may be this way
I have made my prayer sticks into something alive.

—ZUNI PRAYER

MARCH 11

By the grace of God's name
May humanity find itself lifted higher and higher.
In thy dispensation O Lord,
Let there be good in all humanity.

—GURU NANAK

March 12

All hearts are open to You.
All longing is sacred to You.
From you no secret is hidden.
Purify, I beg You, the intentions of my Heart
Through the unspeakable gift of Your grace
So I can love You with all I am
And praise You for all You are.

—Sufi prayer by Andrew Harvey

MARCH 13

Initiator of great virtue, Queen Truth,
May you not thrust
My thinking up against a coarse lie.

—FRIEDRICH HÖLDERLIN

MARCH 14

Lord, enfold me in the depths of your heart; and there
hold me, refine, purge, and set me on fire, raise
me aloft, until my own self knows utter annihilation.

—TEILHARD DE CHARDIN

MARCH 15

O God, from whom all holy desires, all good counsels, and all just works do proceed: Give unto thy servants that peace which the world cannot give, that our hearts may be set to obey thy commandments, and also that by thee, we, being defended from the fear of all enemies, may pass our time in rest and quietness; through the merits of Jesus Christ our Savior. *Amen.*

—THE BOOK OF COMMON PRAYER

MARCH 16

King Zeus, give what is good
Even if not prayed for
And keep far from us evil,
Even though we ask for it.

—ANCIENT GREEK PRAYER

MARCH 17

God grant me the serenity
to accept the things I cannot change;
courage to change the things I can;
and wisdom to know the difference.

—REINHOLD NIEBUHR

MARCH 18

Cease, fierce wind:
Come wind, warm with love's memories
Breathe through my garden
The scent of your caresses,
For the Beloved to graze among the flowers.

—SAINT JOHN OF THE CROSS

MARCH 19

O flame with the honored treasures
Rise and blaze in me!
For you control and support all things
Like a pillar
And the head of Heaven and the Earth!

—THE RIG VEDA

MARCH 20

For those who have come to grow,
The whole world is a garden.
For those who wish to remain in illusion,
The whole world is a stage.
For those who have come to learn,
The whole world is a university.
Make me one of those, Lord, who come to know God
For whom the world becomes their prayer mat.

—ANDREW HARVEY, INSPIRED BY BAWA MUHAIYADDEEN

MARCH 21

May I be like
One of those small children
Who, with one hand,
Hold on to their father,
And, with the other,
Pick strawberries and blackberries
Along the hedges.

—FRANCIS DE SALES

MARCH 22

Beloved, drag me, I beg you
Into the gang of the crazy.
For the ecstasy of drunkenness
Is far more precious to me
Than any sane sobriety.
Do anything you need to me
To drive me mad with Love and set me free.

—RUMI

MARCH 23

O sky above me, pure deep sky! Abyss of light!
Gazing into you, I tremble with divine desires.
May my depth be to toss myself up to your height!
May I learn, like you, to smile down with luminous eyes
Out of miles of distance, while under us
Constraint and empty purpose and guilt steam like rain.
May I, like you, say a vast unbounded Yes and Amen.

—FRIEDRICH NIETZSCHE

March 24

You who are robed
In the most brilliant Lights
Show yourself to me
In the most beautiful
Of epiphanies
Show me Your dazzling Face
Be for me the mediator
Lift the heavy veils of darkness
From my heart.

—Sohravardi

MARCH 25

May I attain the highest void.
May I maintain, without wavering,
The most profound stillness.
As the ten thousand things rise and fall
May I watch their turning back.

—TAOIST PRAYER

MARCH 26

In all my days
Growing up among the sages
I found nothing better than silence.
Heap its burnished gold, Lord
In my heart's holy of holies.

—KABBALISTIC PRAYER

MARCH 27

Let her who seeks
Never cease striving
Until she finds
And when she finds
She will be troubled
And when she has been troubled
She will be amazed
And she will reign over all.

—LOGION 2 THE GOSPEL OF THOMAS

MARCH 28

O my Lord,
If I worship You
From fear of hell, burn me in hell.
If I worship You
From hope of Paradise, bar me from its gates.

But if I worship You
For yourself alone,
Grant me then the beauty of Your face.

—RABIA BASRI

March 29

Say I take refuge with the Lord of humanity
The King of humanity
The God of humanity
From the evil of the slinking whisperer
Who whispers in the breast of humanity
And from spirits and humanity.

—Prayer from the Qur'an (Sura 24)

MARCH 30

Prayer for the White Lions

You are the great beasts of the sun
You are as lovely as blooms that spring from the earth
You are as magnificent as the sun at dawn
O Lions that are white
Make our hearts as great as yours!

—African shamanic prayer

MARCH 31

Mary, teach my whole being
Always to go on saying Yes as you did
So I too can give birth
To the Prince of Peace.

—ANDREW HARVEY, INSPIRED BY MIRABAI STARR

APRIL

APRIL 1

May I, in pursuit of the noble science of alchemy,
Purify my being before God
And wipe away corruption from my heart.
May I transform myself
From a dead stone
Into a living philosophical stone!
May I, child of an exalted line,
Rise from the lowest to the highest
And then unite the darkest in me
With the highest and widest light
And become the One and the many within me.

—ANCIENT ALCHEMIST'S PRAYER

April 2

Longing for you savages me each moment
Let the world be my killer, not you
Don't kick the man you sent sprawling in the dust
Don't kill him you made, for the first time, alive.

—Rumi

APRIL 3

O Lord, on this night
Let no one fall asleep
Except in Your arms
And let no one die
Except to Your infinite Light.

—SUFI PRAYER BY ANDREW HARVEY

APRIL 4

Lord, make of my soul and body
Your luminous house
And amass there
The heavenly riches of Your spirit.

—SAINT MACARIUS

APRIL 5

After my many sufferings and great martyry
May I rise again transfigured, of all blemish free.

—ANCIENT ALCHEMIST'S PRAYER

APRIL 6

O Incomparable Giver of life, cut reason loose at last!
Let it wander gray-eyed from vanity to vanity.
Shatter open my skull, pour in it the wine of madness!
Let me be mad, as You, mad with You, with us.
Beyond the sanity of fools is the burning desert
Where Your sun is whirling in every atom.
Beloved, drag me there, let me roast in Perfection!

—RUMI

APRIL 7

O cheer and tune my heartless breast,
Defer no time;
That so thy favors granting my request,
They and my mind may chime,
And mend my rhyme.

—GEORGE HERBERT

APRIL 8

Death-Bed of a Financier

Deal not with me God as I have dealt with Man
In the prosperity which thou hast given me
Helpless in his need a careless course I ran
And now oh Lord that thou hast driven me
To my last gasp, I pray for all I am not worth
Deal not with me as I have dealt on earth.

—STEVIE SMITH

APRIL 9

O God, grace me love of You, and give me the grace to
Love those who love You, and to love
Whatever brings me nearer to You.

O God, may Your love be more precious to me
Than cool water to the thirsty.

—THE PROPHET MUHAMMAD

APRIL 10

Deliver me from every false passion
From anger, delusion, and all other vice.
Let me bear witness through all my anguish
To a devoted heart and works well done.

—MARY, QUEEN OF SCOTS

APRIL 11

Beloved Pan, and all the other Gods
Who haunt this place—
Grant that I may become inwardly beautiful.

—PLATO, *PHAEDRUS 279*

APRIL 12

Lit up from within by your sacred fire,
Mother, let my heart become a sanctuary
For all the helpless and desolate and broken.
Mother, teach me
To serve all beings ceaselessly as you do,
Serenely, smiling through tears of blood.

—ANDREW HARVEY, INSPIRED BY MIRABAI STARR

APRIL 13

Holy Spirit, pour down on me
Illuminate me, use me
To complete your work on earth.

—CATHOLIC EUCHARIST PRAYER

APRIL 14

Mother, humanity needs you now
To so illuminate our minds and hearts
That we all know
That all religions are roads
That lead to the palace of God
That all paths are many-colored rivers
Rushing, turbid with dogmatism,
To the same eternally shining serene sea.
O Mother, illuminate us now and make us wise.

—SRI RAMAKRISHNA

APRIL 15

Be with me, Lord,
As I wander alone
Under Your stars
With only my longing for You
As my companion.

—HERMANN HESSE

APRIL 16

O God, come to my help!
Lord, hurry to my rescue!

—PSALM 69

APRIL 17

In this age when history itself is on fire
In this time of the convulsion of the beast
Of the final dance of the enraged demons
May I keep faith, Lord, in Your sublime alchemy
That has ordained the mystery
That from deepest darkness births the Highest Light.

—ANDREW HARVEY

APRIL 18

How ridiculous and unrealistic
Is the human being
Who is astonished in this life!
Do with me anything, O Gods
But do not make me one of these!

—MARCUS AURELIUS

APRIL 19

My wild wisdom has become pregnant
In the lonely mountains
Send me the companions
That can help birth her child!

—FRIEDRICH NIETZSCHE

APRIL 20

May I so live that I leave this life full of gratitude for You, for you have judged me worthy of celebrating the festival with you, of contemplating your works, and of following with you the way in which you govern the world.

—EPICTETUS

APRIL 21

Lord I stand before You
Like a stone before a sculptor
And beg You to form Your perfect image in my soul
And make me entirely like You.

—BROTHER LAWRENCE OF THE RESURRECTION

APRIL 22

You are playing your music again
And I run after each golden tone.

Suddenly I ring like a gong struck by God.
Oh, my heart is indestructible whenever You play on it.

Strike me, Beloved, again and again.
Never stop sounding my wild thunder heart.

—Janine Canan

APRIL 23

So burn me through, Beloved
With the infinite fire of Your Love
That I may become your brazier ablaze
With sacred passion for all of creation.

—SUFI PRAYER BY ANDREW HARVEY

APRIL 24

May all my days be holy to me!
This is what joyous wisdom
Is always, always praying in me
May all my days be holy to me.

—FRIEDRICH NIETZSCHE

APRIL 25

With the recognition and remembrance that Samsara
Is a fiery pit, a garden of razors, a forest of swords
May I constantly arouse the most passionate aspiration
To be quickly freed from all illusions and sufferings
So as to be able to guide all beings into Nirvana.

—PADMASAMBHAVA

April 26

May I be so transformed
By your love's wisdom
That I kneel perpetually
At the feet of all creatures.

—Mechthild of Magdeburg

April 27

May I seek authentic teachings
Like a mother hawk seeks her prey.
May I listen to the teachings
Like a deer enchanted by music.
May I meditate on the teachings
Like a beggar relishing bread.
May I contemplate the teachings
Like a northern nomad shearing sheep.
May I attain their highest realization
Like a sun breaking out from dark clouds.

—Padampa Sangye

APRIL 28

Beloved, grace me your endless lavishness
Make me like Your sun
Pouring out life-giving splendor
On good and evil alike.

—RUMI

APRIL 29

Oh Kwan Yin, who sits at ease
Listening to the sounds of the universe
Build your ears in mine
Ground me in your infinite spaciousness
Irradiate me with your skillful means
To help all beings that arise on my path.

—ANDREW HARVEY

APRIL 30

If I were a nightingale
I would sing like a nightingale;
If I were a swan, like a swan.
I am a man gifted with knowledge
So my joy is to praise You, O God of the universe.
This is my task: raise me up
So I can fulfill it.
Give me the courage not to abandon it
So long as it is decreed for me.
Join with me in the song of praise
My heart is always singing to You.

—Epictetus

MAY

MAY 1

May I see and know and serve
Every living being
As the Absolute God.

—SRI RAMAKRISHNA

MAY 2

For everything born
Death is certain.

And for everything that dies
Birth is certain.

May I have the wisdom
Never to grieve
Over the unavoidable.

—MARCUS AURELIUS

MAY 3

Let us build our nest in the tree of the future!
Eagles will bring the lonely food in their beaks!
Let us live like strong winds, neighbors to the eagles,
To the snow, to the sun; let us live like strong free winds!

—FRIEDRICH NIETZSCHE

MAY 4

May I be like the almond tree
That, whether there be cars—
Or no cars—on the winding roads,
Wars or no wars,
Whether there be music in the house or not,
Or famine, or concentration camps,
Or the systematic drowning of billions
In tsunamis of perpetual distraction—
Still brings forth her blossoms in silence.

—ANDREW HARVEY, INSPIRED BY THOMAS MERTON

MAY 5

May I be your riverbed,
Great Stream.

May You keep on flowing
Through me.

May I be strong enough to carry You
Toward your destination.

—JANINE CANAN

MAY 6

O Lord, pour down steadfastness upon us
Make our feet firm
And grant us victory over the hosts of
Darkness.

—SUFI PRAYER

MAY 7

O holy Virgin,
In the midst of your glory,
Do not forget the miseries of this earth.
Cast a merciful glance upon those
Who are struggling with difficulties,
Those who are suffering,
Their lips pressed constantly against
Life's bitter cup.

—SAINT AUGUSTINE

May 8

Lead me back to your green valleys
With the sheep of your flock.
Feed me together with them
On the fresh grazing of the mysteries
Where the pure heart dwells, the heart
That bears in it
The splendor of your revelations.
Lord, through your grace and your love for us,
May we be worthy of your splendor.

—Isaac of Nineveh

MAY 9

O blessed silent one who speaks everywhere!
Speak to me in your tenderest voice
In all sides in everything
So I am never the same again.
Awaken me, not to conquest or dark pleasure,
But to the impeccable pure simplicity
Of one consciousness in all and through all.
Help me express in my own heart
Your clear silence. Make me eternal.

—ADAPTED FROM THOMAS MERTON'S "HAGIA SOPHIA"

MAY 10

All creation is your play, my mad mother Kali
By your Maya are all three worlds bedazzled!
You are crazy and your husband is crazy.
Not even the most illuminated mystic
Could describe your glories, beauty, gestures, moods.
May I be like Shiva, with the poison in his throat,
Chanting your name again and again!

—SRI RAMAKRISHNA

MAY 11

May heartbreak for you
Reveal a treasure in my heart!
May my heart become "light upon light"
Mary with Jesus leaping in her womb.

—RUMI

MAY 12

Divine Mother, give me Your eyes so I can see myself
through them and see how holy in Your eyes is my soul,
and how holy in Your eyes is my heart, and how holy
and sacred in Your eyes is my body. Help me be as
merciful and generous with myself as You would always
want me to be. Help me honor myself as I have found to
my amazement You honor me. Help me live and work
from the peace and balance and compassion from which
You live and work. Help me in these ways, Mother, so I
can at last truly become the instrument you need me to
become, the sacred instrument of Your compassion in
action, that You created me to be, and that I already am
in Your holy and illumined eyes.

—ANDREW HARVEY

MAY 13

May He Grant Us the Grace of His Beauty

May the field of the heart be opened wide
May we see Reality's light
May we taste the wine of His fervent love
Granting us the grace of His Beauty.

—UFTADE

MAY 14

Collects: Contemporary, "Of a Saint"

Almighty God, you have surrounded us with a
great cloud of witnesses: Grant that we, encouraged
by their good example, may persevere in running the
race that is set before us, until at least we may with them
attain to your eternal joy; through Jesus Christ, the
pioneer and perfector of our faith, who lives and reigns
with you and the Holy Spirit, on God, for ever and ever.
Amen.

—THE BOOK OF COMMON PRAYER

MAY 15

Mother of God, save me.

—ANCIENT RUSSIAN ORTHODOX PRAYER

MAY 16

Mother, our world is burning.
I will stand beside you.
Together we will usher an age of peace and
Mercy
Back into the broken heart of the creation.
Together we will step into the flames
And we will not be consumed.

—ANDREW HARVEY, INSPIRED BY MIRABAI STARR

MAY 17

May I be one of the illumined ones
Who sees the body
As the temple of Shiva
And so realize the Great Bliss
Of transforming its every activity
Into worship and ecstasy.

—ABHINAVAGUPTA

MAY 18

From today onward
Until the attainment of enlightenment
May I be willing
To live with my chaos and confusion
And that of all other sentient beings.
May I be willing
To share our mutual confusion
And work incessantly and humbly
To help and elevate everyone without exception.

—TIBETAN PRAYER

MAY 19

I am unreal!
My heart is unreal!
My devotion is unreal!
Sinner as I am,
I can attain Thee if I but cry for Thee!
O Sweet Lord!
O Honey!
O Clear Juice of the Sugar Cane!
Be gracious, that I may reach Thee!

—MANIKKAVACHAKAR

MAY 20

If the storms of temptation arise,
If you crash against the rocks of tribulation,
Look to the star, call upon Mary.
If you toss about on the waves of pride, of ambition, of
slander, of hostility,
Look to the star, call upon Mary.
If you begin to be swallowed up by the abyss of
depression and despair,
Think of Mary!
In dangers, in anxiety, in doubt,
Think of Mary, call upon Mary . . . When you are
terrified by judgment or in despair, think of Mary
For if she holds you, you will never fail.
If she protects you, you need not fear.
May I, O Mary, always remember those words.

—ANDREW HARVEY, INSPIRED BY BERNARD DE CLAIRVAUX

MAY 21

Lord, send me staggering with the wine
Of Your love!
Ring my feet
With the chains of Your slavery!
Empty me of everything but Your love
And in it destroy and resurrect me!
Any hunger You awaken
Can only end in feast!

—SHEIKH ANSARI

May 22

May the axe be far away from you;
May the fire be far away from you;
May there be rain without storm;
Lord of Trees, may you be blessed;
Lord of Trees, may you be blessed.

—HINDU PRAYER

May 23

May the earth continue to live;
May the heavens above continue to live;
May the rains continue to dampen the land;
May the wet forests continue to grow;
Then the flowers shall bloom
And we people shall live again.

—Hawaiian prayer

MAY 24

I reverently speak in the presence
of the Great Parent God:

I give you grateful thanks
That you have enabled me to live this day,
The whole day,
In obedience to the excellent spirit of your ways.

—SHINTO PRAYER

MAY 25

If You were to place before me hellfire, with all it
contains of torment,
I would think lightly of it in comparison with my state
when You are hidden from me.
Forgive the people and do not forgive me.
Have mercy upon them and do not have mercy upon me.
I do not intercede with You for myself or beseech You
for what is due to me.
Do with me what you will.

—MANSUR AL-HALLAJ, BEFORE HIS EXECUTION

MAY 26

May I relinquish myself and embrace reality
And do what needs to be done.

—ANDREW HARVEY, INSPIRED BY RABBI SHEMAYA

MAY 27

Prayer of the Farm Workers' Struggle

Show me the suffering of the most miserable;
So I will know my people's plight.

Free me to pray for others;
For you are present in every person.

Help me take responsibility for my own life;
So that I can be free at last.

Grant me courage to serve others;
For in service there is true life.

Give me honesty and patience;
So that I can work with other workers.

Bring forth song and celebration;
So that the Spirit will be alive among us.

Let the Spirit flourish and grow;
So that we will never tire of the struggle.

Let us remember those who have died for justice;
For they have given us life.

Help us love even those who hate us;
So we can change the world.

Amen.

—César E. Chávez

MAY 28

O my soul, may I know in you
Every sun and night, every silence and longing,
So you can grow up in me like a vine
With swelling udders and clusters of golden grapes.

—FRIEDRICH NIETZSCHE

MAY 29

O Lord, remember not only
the men and women of good will
but also those of evil will.
But remember not all the suffering
they have inflicted upon us;
remember the fruits we have borne
thanks to this suffering—
our comradeship, our loyalty,
our humility,
our courage, our generosity,
the greatness of heart
which has grown out of all of this;
and when they come
to stand before you
let these speak for them.

—ANONYMOUS PRAYER FOUND IN RAVENSBRÜCK
CONCENTRATION CAMP

MAY 30

Hammer this heart any way you like
For the right ringing sounds
To spread like water
Over the dry listening dead.

—RUMI

MAY 31

Let us adore the Lord,
Maker of marvelous works,
Bright heaven with its angels,
And on the earth the white-waved sea.

—CELTIC PRAYER

JUNE

June 1

Lord Jesus, my Divine Master,
Who wept for Lazarus,
And shed for him tears of grief and compassion,
Accept the tears of my bitterness.
By your sufferings assuage my sufferings.
By your wounds heal my wounds.
By your blood purify my blood.
Pour out on my body
The fragrance of your life-giving body.

—Isaac of Nineveh

JUNE 2

Prayer to Wisdom

Girl-child, you are always
Playing in the world
Obvious and unseen,
Playing at all times before the creator.
Take off my rags of awful solemnity,
Of doubt, of rabid self-absorption
So I can be naked to your joy
And see all things and beings as they are—
Laughing and dancing already at the wedding feast.

—ANDREW HARVEY, INSPIRED BY THOMAS MERTON

June 3

O Lord,
May I always live in awe of You
And cleave to the company
Of those who are sincere.

—SUFI PRAYER

JUNE 4

My boat is tiny and is laden with stones.
Eddies are tossing it from all sides
And the helmsman is drunk
And the boat is midstream.
There is a whirlwind, and on top of it all
Rain is pouring in torrents.
Girdhar the poet says,
O Lord, be the helmsman.
Let your mercy be the oar,
And let the boat reach the shore safe.

—GIRIDHAR GAMANG

JUNE 5

Lord, grace me from you
The most complete receptivity
So I can receive from you
Your most holy effusion.

—Ibn Arabi

JUNE 6

O Hidden Life, vibrant in every atom!
O Hidden Light, shining in every creature!
O Hidden Love, embracing all in oneness!
May each, who feels himself as one with Thee,
Know he is also one with every other.

—ANNIE BESANT

June 7

Sub tuum praesidium

Mother of God, we fly to you
Our shade and shelter
On our pilgrim's way.
Look tenderly on our prayers
And turn not from us
In our time of need
But free us
From the dangers that beset us,
Radiant and Holy Virgin.

—ANONYMOUS

JUNE 8

O our Father, the Sky, hear us
And make us strong.
O our Mother the earth, hear us
And give us support.
O Spirit of the East,
Send us your wisdom.
O Spirit of the South,
May we tread your path of life.
O Spirit of the West,
May we always be ready for the long journey.
O Spirit of the North, purify us
With your cleansing winds.

—SIOUX PRAYER

JUNE 9

What would the world be, once bereft
Of wet and wildness? Let them be left,
O let them be left, wildness and wet;
Long live the weeds and the wilderness yet.

—GERARD MANLEY HOPKINS

June 10

Oh My Guardian Angel

Oh my guardian Angel, whom I left
when I discovered, with a prodigal foot, the forest's gold:
I am poor today. Take my hand in yours.

Oh my guardian Angel, whom I left
when I dreamed before the snowy rooftops:
I no longer know how to dream. Take my hand in yours.

—Francis Jammes

JUNE 11

Beloved Lord, Almighty God!
Through the rays of the sun,
Through the waves of the air,
Through the All-pervading Life in space,
Purify and revivify me, and, I pray,
Heal my body, heart, and soul. Amen.

—HAZRAT INAYAT KHAN

June 12

We place ourselves in your keeping, holy Mother of God.
Hear the prayer of your children in their distress and
protect us from all danger,
O you who are so blessed.

—Anonymous

JUNE 13

O Beloved,
Do not let me pray for the poor
Without working tirelessly
To end the systems that thrive on poverty.
Do not let me pray for the animals
Without working to end
The systems that are slaughtering them.
Do not let me pray for justice and compassion
And the coming of your kingdom
Without being willing to give my life
To make them real.
Save me from the subtle and lethal hypocrisy
That would make me believe I love you
When I risk nothing
To make this love real in your world.

—ANDREW HARVEY

JUNE 14

May the Ocean of Essence, the Ocean of
Honey, the Ocean of Wine, the Ocean
Of Ghee, the Ocean of Curd, the
Ocean of Milk, the Ocean of Sweet Water
Sprinkle me with their
Consecrated waters.

—MAHANIRVANA TANTRA

JUNE 15

May the wind blow sweetness,
The rivers flow sweetness,
The herbs grow sweetness,
For the People of Truth!

Sweet be the night,
Sweet the dawn,
Sweet the earth's fragrance,
Sweet be our heaven!

—THE RIG VEDA

JUNE 16

Grandfather,
Look at our brokenness.
We know that in all creation
Only the human family
Has strayed from the Sacred Way.
We know that we are the ones
Who are divided
And we are the ones
Who must come back together
To walk the Sacred Way.
Grandfather,
Sacred One,
Teach us love, compassion, and honor
That we may heal the earth
And heal each other.

—OJIBWAY PRAYER

JUNE 17

O my God and my Creator;
Although You afflict me
With torments of every kind,
It is nothing in comparison
With being far from You!
And though You bless me
With all the wealth of heaven,
It would still be less than the ecstasy
Your love has showered on my heart.

—ROQIYAH, SUFI WOMAN OF THE 13TH CENTURY

JUNE 18

Father in Heaven! When the thought of Thee wakes in our hearts, let it not awaken like a frightened bird that flies in dismay, but like a child waking from its sleep with a heavenly smile.

—SØREN KIERKEGAARD

JUNE 19

Lord, I do not want any more to be only your friend.
For a friend makes only loving but reasoned ascents to you.
I want to be your child and pray to lose my life on the
summits of that simplicity which does not know itself.
I pray to become in my ascent toward you so simple
That your naked simple love can lay hold of me,
So I cease finally, and all my human self dies into your
Divine one. O Lord of all being, make me one of the
hidden children of God.

—ANDREW HARVEY, INSPIRED BY JAN VAN RUYSBROECK

June 20

O Pallas Athena
Sea-born Queen
May you and your Father Zeus
Keep this city and its citizens
From discord and from all calamity
And from untimely death.

—Ancient prayer for Athens

JUNE 21

Prayer to Praise God

God, calm my heart, calm my poor heart,
and on this summer day when a torpor spreads
like water over everything equally,
give me, once again, the courage to praise
you, my God—like the cicada's cry bursting
from the dormant pine—with humility and grace.

—FRANCIS JAMMES

JUNE 22

You have made us for Yourself, O Lord
And our hearts are restless
Until they rest in You.
Deliver us from the noise
Of all our warring selves
So, at last, they rest in Your Peace.

—SAINT AUGUSTINE

JUNE 23

God, illuminate our hearts with your light
And warm up our souls.

—ANCIENT RUSSIAN PRAYER

June 24

Mother, give me always more and more love,
More and more faith, more and more surrender.
Let my soul in its journey into you
Never rest anywhere.
Your love is an infinite expansion.
Expand me infinitely.

—Andrew Harvey

June 25

Lord, as you will and know best, have mercy.

—Saint Macarius

June 26

The most high has wounded me
With his spirit
And filled me with his love,
And his wounding has become my salvation.
Glory to you, O God,
You who are forever the joy of paradise.
Alleluia! Alleluia!

—*The Odes of Solomon*

JUNE 27

May my heart absorb you
And you absorb my heart
So we two become one
In blissful union.

—SAINT JOHN CHRYSOSTOM

JUNE 28

May I be brought by divine grace
To know and experience
God in the world, and the world in God

—MIKHAIL BULGAKOV

JUNE 29

Paul's Prayer for the Ephesians

I ask that Christ will live in your hearts through faith.
As a result of having strong roots in love, I ask that
you'll have the power to grasp love's width and length,
height and depth, together with all believers. I ask that
you'll know the love of Christ that is beyond knowledge
so that you will be filled entirely with the fullness of
God.

—EPHESIANS 3:17–19

JUNE 30

This is your body, Mother,
It is not mine.

Flood every cell
With your resplendent Joy.

—Janine Canan

JULY

JULY 1

Breath of compassion, five-pointed star
Breathe down on me from Your eternal sky
So I may radiate Your tender humility
And enter Your radiance when I die.

—SUFI PRAYER BY ANDREW HARVEY

July 2

Lord if there was one grace I could beg of You
It would be that in every state and station
My soul could keep up with You unbroken conversation.

—Brother Lawrence of the Resurrection

July 3

May I be taken, Mother,
Into your great light
And see all beings' faces bright as stars
All places bright as if they are wearing
The full moon as a dress
And all the night's dark expanses
Vivid as the morning sun.
May I know there is no death, no day or night,
That life is eternally one, one, one.

—SRI RAMAKRISHNA

JULY 4

Lord, in our lives there are hours completely covered in darkness, sad hours in which the veil cast over the heart hides even those that could comfort us, in which we suffer in a way that nothing on earth can save us.

In such hours, Lord, may our weak hands still clasp Your feet on the cross: may our weary hands still lean against Your pierced hands: may our shattered hearts press against Yours, that has suffered so infinitely and still always blazes with compassion and hope for all.

—ELISABETH LESEUR

JULY 5

O Give what you demand, Lord!

—SAINT AUGUSTINE

JULY 6

Lost in the desert between
True awareness and the senses
May I suddenly wake inside myself
Like a lotus blossoming
In water weeds.

—LALLA

JULY 7

The sea of bitterness, the sea of sweetness—
In this world there is a wall between them.
Yet both seas, I know, flow from one origin:
May I cross both of them to reach that shore.

—RUMI

JULY 8

O Lord,
Let me understand You.
I cannot understand from You
Except through You.

—ABU YAZID BISTAMI

July 9

I pray for the gift of silence,
Of emptiness and solitude,
Where everything I touch is turned into prayer:
Where the sky is my prayer
The birds are my prayer,
The wind in the trees is my prayer,
For you are all in all.

—Andrew Harvey, inspired by Thomas Merton

July 10

O my God,
My work and desire
In this world
Is remembering You
And in the next,
Meeting with You.
This is what is mine—
You do as You will.

—Rabia Basri

JULY 11

Our Lord, do not lay it to our charge when we forget
and are at fault. Our Lord, what would be more than
we could carry do not lay upon us. Rather, grant us
pardon, forgive us, and have mercy on us. For You are
our Sovereign. Be our aid against those who hold You in
contempt.

—MUSLIM PRAYER

July 12

Bestow, O God, this grace on us, that in the school of
suffering we should learn self-conquest,
And through sorrow, even if it be against our will, learn
self-control.

—AESCHYLUS

July 13

Dear Ahura Mazda,
I begin this day with Your Holy Name.
Help me to spend it usefully.

—Zoroastrian prayer

JULY 14

Flame of love
Irradiate my heart.
Flame of beauty
Illumine my soul.
Flame of wisdom
Exalt my mind.
Flame of courage
Impassion my will.
Flame of peace
Steady my being.

—ANDREW HARVEY

JULY 15

From the confusing tumult of Becoming,
lead me steadily,
Upward and onward,
A wandering soul, to the holy light.

—PROCLUS

July 16

In Thy image let me pattern my life, O Ahura Mazda.
Let me awake with Thy name on my lips.
In my eyes let me ever carry Thy image
To enable me to perceive Thee,
And Thee alone, in everyone else.

—Zoroastrian prayer

July 17

From silly devotions
And from sour-faced saints,
Good Lord, deliver us.

—Teresa of Ávila

July 18

A Prayer of Surrender

Take, Lord, all my liberty
My memory, my understanding,
And my whole will.
You have given me all that I have
All that I am,
And I surrender to your divine will,
That you dispose of me.
Give me only your love and your grace.
With this I am rich enough,
And I have no more to ask.

—Saint Ignatius of Loyola

July 19

Let my impatient love overflow in golden streams
Out of silent mountains and storms of affliction
Let my soul rush out to fertilize new valleys!

—Friedrich Nietzsche

July 20

Holy Spirit
think through me
till your ideas
are my ideas.

—Amy Carmichael

July 21

Prayer for the Animals

Hear our humble prayer, O God, for our friends the animals. We entreat for them all your mercy and pity, and for those who deal with them we ask a heart of compassion, gentle hands, and kindly words.
Make us ourselves to be true friends to animals and so to share the blessing of the merciful. For the sake of your Son, the tender-hearted Jesus Christ our Lord.

—ANGLICAN COLLECT

JULY 22

May the road rise to meet you,
May the wind be always at your back,
May the sun shine warm on your face,
The rain fall softly on your fields;
And until we meet again,
May God hold you in the palm of his hand.

—GAELIC BLESSING

JULY 23

May I be lifted up
Into the wisdom of emptiness
And so make my giving to all beings perfect
And become like a water crystal jewel,
Destroying, by irradiating, darkness!

—ANDREW HARVEY, INSPIRED BY SHANTIDEVA

July 24

Lord, let me not live to be useless.

—John Wesley

July 25

O Lord God, grant us always, whatever the world may say, to content ourselves with what thou wilt say, and to care only for thine approval, which will outweigh all words.

—General Charles George Gordon

JULY 26

O Lord, help me not to despise or oppose what I do not understand.

—WILLIAM PENN

JULY 27

After so many sufferings, diseases, troubles, and pains
May I, and all humanity, return humbly to the one being
And enter that city whose citizens rejoice in Being itself.

—SAINT AUGUSTINE

JULY 28

O Lord God, when thou givest to thy servants to endeavor any great matter, grant us also to know that it is not the beginning, but the continuing of the same to the end, until it be thoroughly finished, which yieldeth the true glory; through him who for the finishing of thy work laid down his life, our Redeemer, Jesus Christ.

—SIR FRANCIS DRAKE

JULY 29

O Jesus,
Be the canoe that holds me in the sea of life.
Be the steer that keeps me straight.
Be the outrigger that supports me in times of
great temptation.
Let your Spirit be my sail that carries me through
each day.
Keep my body strong,
So that I can paddle steadfastly on,
In the long voyage of life.

—NEW HEBRIDEAN PRAYER

July 30

Teach me, my God and King,
In all things thee to see,
And what I do in any thing,
To do it as for thee.

—George Herbert

JULY 31

Courage my Soul, now learn to wield
The weight of thine immortal Shield.
Close on thy Head thy Helmet bright.
Balance thy Sword against the Fight.
See where an Army, strong as fair,
With silken Banners spreads the air.
Now, if thou bee'st that thing Divine,
In this day's Combat let it shine:
And show that Nature wants an Art
To conquer one resolved Heart.

—ANDREW MARVELL

AUGUST

AUGUST 1

On that day the mountains shall pass like clouds
And the creation fold up like a fan.
Let me rise from my grave singing Your name
Ablaze in the fire of Your mercy.

—SUFI PRAYER BY ANDREW HARVEY

AUGUST 2

I do not know where lead the paths;
The end of the road is out of view.
May it be enough for me to know
That Love will see my footsteps through.

—GHALIB

AUGUST 3

Return, O Dove,
So the wounded stag
Rises over the horizon's dawn
Refreshed by the wind of your flight.

—SAINT JOHN OF THE CROSS

AUGUST 4

Lord, Thou knowest better than I know myself that I am
growing older and will someday be old. Keep me from
the fatal habit of thinking I must say something on every
subject and on every occasion. Release me from the craving
to straighten out everybody's affairs. Make me thoughtful
but not moody, helpful but not bossy. With my vast store of
wisdom, it seems a pity not to use it all, but Thou knowest,
Lord that I want a few friends in the end.

Keep my mind free of recital of endless details; give me
wings to get to the point. Seal my lips on my aches and
pains. They are increasing, and my love of rehearsing
them is becoming sweeter as the years go by. I dare not
ask for the grace to enjoy the tales of others' pain, but help
me to endure them with patience.

I dare not ask for improved memory, but for a growing
humility and a lessening cocksureness when my memory
seems to clash with the memories of others. Teach me the
glorious lesson that occasionally I may be mistaken.

Keep me reasonably sweet; I do not want to be a Saint—
some of them are so hard to live with—but a sour old
person is one of the crowning works of the devil.

Give me the ability to see good things in unexpected
places, and talents in unexpected people. And give me,
Lord, the grace to tell them so. Amen.

—17th-CENTURY NUN

AUGUST 5

O blessed Lord, you ministered to all who came to you: Look with compassion upon all who through addiction have lost their health and freedom. Restore to them the assurance of your unfailing mercy; remove from them the fears that beset them; strengthen them in the work of their recovery; and to those who care for them, give patience, understanding, and persevering love. *Amen.*

—THE BOOK OF COMMON PRAYER

AUGUST 6

O Lord, you have made us very small, and we bring our years to an end like a tale that is told; help us to remember that beyond our brief day is the eternity of your love.

—REINHOLD NEIBUHR

AUGUST 7

My enemies have called me a fool and a liar
As they have slandered better men before me.
Lord, help me always find forgiveness in my soul
So, whatever my enemies may do, I remain whole.

—SUFI PRAYER BY ANDREW HARVEY

AUGUST 8

O Mother, You walk the streets in one form and exist in
the universe in another.
Above all else I greet You, O Mother.

—SWAMI VIVEKANANDA

AUGUST 9

I Would Not Even Care To Be an Emperor

Mother of the Universe,
I have no desire to exercise power.
I would not even care to be an emperor.
Sweet Mother, please grant me
two simple meals each day
and wealth enough to thatch the palm roof
of my clean earthen house,
where I offer dreaming and waking
as red flowers at your feet.

My green village dwelling is the abode
of your golden radiance, O Goddess.
What need have I for more elaborate construction?
If you surround me with the complex architecture
of stature and possession,
I will refuse to call you *Mother* ever again.

—RAMPRASAD SEN

AUGUST 10

The wrong of ignorance, the wrong of thoughtlessness,
The wrong of not having followed Thee with a melting
heart,
The wrong of not having meditated upon Thee,
The wrong of not having prayed and worshipped Thee,
O Supreme Almighty, forgive me of all my wrongs!

—PATTINATHAR

AUGUST 11

O my Lord, let security and truth precede and follow me
wherever You lead me.
Let authority and succor from Your presence be with me.

— THE PROPHET MUHAMMAD

AUGUST 12

Breughel

The ages blaspheme
The people are weak
As in a dream
They evilly speak.

Their words in a clatter
Of meaningless sound
Without form or matter
Echo around.

The people oh Lord
Are sinful and sad
Prenatally biassed
Grow worser born bad

They sicken oh Lord
They have no strength in them
Oh rouse up my God
And against their will win them.

Must thy lambs to the slaughter
Delivered be
With each son and daughter
Irrevocably?

From tower and steeple
Ring out funeral bells
Oh Lord save thy people
They have no help else.

—STEVIE SMITH

AUGUST 13

The Song of the Sun

Glory to You, my Lord, for sister moon and the stars
You have made in heaven clear, precious, and beautiful.
Glory to You, my Lord, for brother wind
And for air and cloud and serene sky
And all the different weathers
By which You sustain all creatures.
Glory to You, my Lord, for sister water
Who is very useful and humble
And precious and pure.
Glory to You, my Lord for brother fire
By whom You illumine night
And he is beautiful and joyful and robust and full of
power.
Glory to You, my Lord for sister our mother earth
Who sustains and governs us
And produces different fruits
And brightly colored flowers and grass.

—SAINT FRANCIS OF ASSISI

AUGUST 14

Grant me peace and return,
For I am ruined by your leaving.

—HAFIZ

AUGUST 15

Against every new outrage
And every new horror
May we put up
One more piece of love and goodness
Drawing deeper and deeper strength
From within our deepest selves.

—ANDREW HARVEY, INSPIRED BY ETTY HILLESUM

AUGUST 16

Cure thy children's warring madness;
Bend our pride to thy control;
Shame our wanton selfish gladness,
Rich in things and poor in soul.
Grant us wisdom, grant us courage,
Lest we miss thy Kingdom's goal,
Lest we miss thy Kingdom's goal.

—HARRY EMERSON FOSDICK

AUGUST 17

Prayer to Confess One's Ignorance

Glory is vain, oh my God, and so is genius.
It is yours alone—to bestow upon humanity,
who unknowingly repeat the same words
like a swarm of summer bees among dark branches.
As I rise this morning from my table, help me
to be like those who on this beautiful Sunday
will offer at your feet, in a humble white church,
the pure and modest confession of their simple ignorance.

—FRANCIS JAMMES

AUGUST 18

In the name of Allah; I place my trust in Allah! O Allah,
I seek refuge in You from being made to stumble, from
straying and from being made to stray, for doing wrong
to others and from being wronged by others, and from
misunderstanding and from being misunderstood.

—The Prophet Muhammad

AUGUST 19

O my mother Nut,
stretch your wings over me.
Let me become like the imperishable stars,
like the indefatigable stars.

—ANCIENT EGYPTIAN PRAYER

AUGUST 20

All that we ought to have thought and have not thought,
All that we ought to have said and have not said,
All that we ought to have done and have not done;

All that we ought not to have thought and yet have
thought,
All that we ought not to have spoken and yet have spoken,
All that we ought not to have done and yet have done;
For thoughts, words, and works, pray we, O God, for
forgiveness.

—ANCIENT PERSIAN PRAYER

August 21

God bless all those that I love;
God bless all those that love me;
God bless all those that love those that I love
And all those that love those that love me.

—ANONYMOUS

AUGUST 22

Let nothing disturb you;
Let nothing dismay you;
All things pass:
God never changes.
Patience attains
All it strives for.
He who loves God
Finds he lacks nothing:
God alone suffices.

—TERESA OF ÁVILA

AUGUST 23

Drop thy still dews of quietness,
Till all our strivings cease;
Take from our souls the strain and stress,
And let our ordered lives confess
The beauty of thy peace.

—JOHN GREENLEAF WHITTIER

AUGUST 24

May I always remember
Neither condemnation nor hatred
Will bring me closer to my sacred goal
But only patient love and loving patience.

—ANDREW HARVEY, INSPIRED BY HERMANN HESSE

AUGUST 25

Blessed are you all, poor, hungry, sick,
And hopeless. My Father, giver of life,
Holds you in His heart. He will inaugurate
His kingdom of Life, of Justice, of
Tenderness, and of Freedom, and you will
Be its first inhabitants.

—LEONARDO BOFF

AUGUST 26

Come, my Light, and illumine my darkness.
Come, my Life, and revive me from death.
Come, my Physician, and heal my wounds.
Come, Flame of divine love, and burn up
the thorns of my sins, kindling
My heart with the flame of thy love.
Come, my King, sit upon the throne of my heart
and reign there.
For thou alone art my King and my Lord.

—SAINT DIMITRY OF ROSTOV

AUGUST 27

O burning mountain, O chosen sun,
O perfect moon, O fathomless well,
O unattainable height, O clearness beyond measure,
O wisdom without end, O mercy without limit,
O strength beyond resistance, O crown of all majesty,
Grace that I may always sing your praise.

—MECHTHILD OF MAGDEBURG

August 28

We gather our minds together to send greetings and thanks to all the animal life in the world.

They have many things to teach us as people. We see them near our homes and in the deep forests.

We are glad they are still here and we hope that it will always be so.

Now our minds are one.

—Native American prayer

AUGUST 29

May I know love and cherish it, May I know sorrow and embrace it,

May I know happiness and be enchanted, May I know forgiveness and feel it.

May I know poverty and heal it.

May I know richness and give it away.

May I know wisdom and seek it, May I know music and dance it.

May I know despair and enter it, May I know heaviness and walk through it.

May I shed tears and feel empty, May I know joy, so that I can shine.

May I know darkness so that I can pray.

May I know pain so that I may heal.

May I know shadow so that I become light.

May I know life so I may die into your arms, everlasting. Amen.

—LILLY WHITE

AUGUST 30

The Passionate Man's Pilgrimage

Give me my scallop shell of quiet,
My staff of faith to walk upon,
My scrip of joy, immortal diet,
My bottle of salvation;
My gown of glory, hope's true gage,
And thus I'll take my pilgrimage.

—SIR WALTER RALEIGH

AUGUST 31

May I become one of the patient and forgiving.
May I become one of those who dare to believe
When catastrophe strikes and the worlds burn
To God we belong and to God we return.

—SUFI PRAYER BY ANDREW HARVEY

SEPTEMBER

SEPTEMBER 1

Song of the Sun

Glory to You, my Lord,
For those who forgive for love of You,
And bear sicknesses and ordeals.
Happy are those who bear them in peace
For they will be crowned by You, most high Lord.

—SAINT FRANCIS OF ASSISI

September 2

My Lord and my God,
Take everything from me
That keeps me from Thee.

My Lord and my God
Give everything to me
That brings me near to Thee.

My Lord and my God,
Take me away from myself
And give me completely to Thee.

—Saint Nicholas of Flüe, "Brother Klaus"

SEPTEMBER 3

Abba, Father, all things are possible to thee; remove this cup from me; yet not what I will but what thou wilt.

—Jesus' prayer in Gethsemane

September 4

Mother,
Make of my heart
A vast bed of peace
Where you can lay down your heart
And rest from the agony that harrows it
From all we are and continue to do.
As you comfort me, so may I comfort you.

—Andrew Harvey

September 5

O Giver of stability and sustenance,
Set free mankind from uncertainty and doubt.
In work which is worthy of performance,
Let them be steadfast and certain.
Give them patience and weigh down their scales
And set them free from all vile deceivers.

—Rumi

SEPTEMBER 6

Teach me thy love to know;
That this new light, which now I see,
May both the work and workman be:
Then by a sunbeam I will climb to thee.

—GEORGE HERBERT

September 7

Make me happy as without you I am sad.

—13TH-CENTURY IRAQI SUFI POET

SEPTEMBER 8

There is in God (some say)
A deep, but dazzling darkness;
As men here
Say it is late and dusky, because they
See not all clear
O for that night where I in him
Might live invisible and dim.

—HENRY VAUGHAN

SEPTEMBER 9

Lord Creator, and all you His assistants, help us to be able to remember ourselves at all times in order that we may avoid involuntary actions, as only through them can evil manifest itself.

—GEORGE GURDJIEFF

SEPTEMBER 10

Before thee, Father,
In righteousness and humility,
With thee, Brother,
In faith and courage,
In thee, Spirit,
In stillness.

—DAG HAMMARSKJÖLD

SEPTEMBER 11

In order to come to taste everything,
May I lose my taste in everything.

In order to arrive at what I do not know,
May I go by a way I do not know.

In order to arrive at what I am not,
May I go through the way in which I am not.

—ANDREW HARVEY, INSPIRED BY SAINT JOHN OF THE
CROSS

September 12

Dearest Lord, teach me to be generous;
Teach me to serve thee as thou deserves,
To give and not to count the cost,
To fight and not to heed the wounds,
To toil and not to seek for rest,
To labor and not to seek reward,
Save that of knowing that I do thy will.

—Saint Ignatius of Loyola

SEPTEMBER 13

Lord, when we are wrong,
make us willing to change.
And when we are right,
make us easy to live with.

—PETER MARSHALL

September 14

May the great mystery make sunrise in our hearts.

—Sioux prayer

SEPTEMBER 15

Batter my heart, three person'd God; for, you
As yet, but knock, breathe, shine, and seek to mend;
That I may rise, and stand, o'erthrow me, and bend
Your force, to break, blow, burn, and make me new.

—JOHN DONNE

September 16

The Prophet Complains

Lord, how long will I call for help
and you not listen?
I cry out to you, "Violence!"
but you don't deliver us.
Why do you show me injustice
and look at anguish
so that devastation and violence
are before me?

—Habakkuk 1:1–3

SEPTEMBER 17

Lord Shiva, I pray to you
For undying love.
I pray to you for the birthless state.
But if I am to be born again
I pray for the grace
Of remembering you always.
Still more I pray
To be always at your feet,
Singing in ecstacy while you dance.

—TIRUMULAR

September 18

May I, as this your solitude deepens around me,
Not be afraid of what I am losing—
The friends, the desires, the fantasies of achievement—
So I can come naked into Your arms.

—Andrew Harvey

September 19

O Autumn leaf, be still and yield
When the wind wants to take you away.
Do not resist, be a player in the game.
Surrender to the dancing changes.
Let yourself be broken, seized,
And blown to your next home.

—Hermann Hesse

September 20

O God show me things as they are.

—The Prophet Muhammad

September 21

Unchain my soul O Lord
Let me accept the defeats that have sculpted my journey.
Let me learn that I can endure the fight for the freedom
of my spirit
Let me offer my spirit's passion as a sweet and sacred
offering to you.
Let me free your presence in me.
You long to dream through me
You long to create through me
Let me dare open wide my chest
So that your vigor can flow through me.
Let my freedom be a worship
Let my freedom be for love's sake.
I desire to be free and consumed by your love
I pray Amen.

—Chris Saade

September 22

Let justice be done, though the heavens fall.

—Jim Garrison, from *JFK* by Oliver Stone

SEPTEMBER 23

May my soul learn to stay with attention and loving patience in God with total quietude, achieving nothing through imaginings or its own workings; here, all its faculties are at rest so You, O Divine Beloved, can work what wonders You will in them.

—SAINT JOHN OF THE CROSS

SEPTEMBER 24

Make of my heart, O heart of the universe,
A divine bird that nests only on the throne of God.

—RUMI

SEPTEMBER 25

Prayer to Murugan

With the whole earth
As the lamp
The vast oceans as oil
The sun with its blazing rays
As the flame
I have strung a garland of words
For the feet of the Lord
Who carries the red flaming discus.
Help me, king of kings,
Across this fierce sea of pain.

—ANDREW HARVEY, INSPIRED BY POIGAI ALVAR

September 26

Eternal Father I pray to you from the core of my heart and with all the Powers of my soul that You stream to me from the innermost and most sacred depths of Your Father's heart an ever indwelling nature, life, vision, speech, and activity, so I may at all times be shut up in You and abide in You.

—Meister Eckhart

SEPTEMBER 27

Encage me in Love
So I may learn
With the interior palate of my heart
To taste how sweet it is
To live and bathe and be dissolved in Love,
Going beyond myself in ecstasy.
Let me sing the hymn of Love
Let my soul be lost in Your praise, jubilant in Love.

—THOMAS À KEMPIS

SEPTEMBER 28

O unstained Light,
Gleam of a flower in full bloom,
Teacher, honey-sweet God-food,
Loosener of all charms, cataract of tenderness,
Reveal Yourself to me in me and set me free!

—MANIKKAVACHAKAR

SEPTEMBER 29

O Love, Love, when will you lead my soul
Out of this prison and deliver it
From the chains of the dying body?
When will you lead me into my bridegroom's chamber
Where I can be united with him in ecstasy?
Love, hasten my nuptials: for You
I would die a thousand deaths to live such bliss!

—SAINT GERTRUDE OF HELFTA

SEPTEMBER 30

Make my calamity, Lord, my Providence
Outwardly, it is fire and vengeance
Help me see inwardly it is light and mercy.

—BAHÁ'ULLÁH

OCTOBER

October 1

He made himself like me
So I might receive him.
May I receive him.
He made himself like me
So I may be clothed in him.
May I have no fear when I see him
For his nature is mercy.
He took my nature
So I may understand him.
He has my face:
May I never turn my face from him.

—ANDREW HARVEY, INSPIRED BY *THE ODES OF SOLOMON*

OCTOBER 2

So many blessings, Lord . . .
Make me vast enough to receive them.
Help me harvest the golden fields
They have burnished with rain.

—RUMI

OCTOBER 3

I Love You, I Love You
Is all that I can say.
It is my vision in the night
My dream in the day
The blessing when I pray.
I Love You, I Love You
Is all that I can say.

—BABA FARID

OCTOBER 4

He who is not my friend: may God be his.
He who harbors malice against me: may his joys
increase.
He who, as my enemy, scatters thorns in my path:
May each flower in his life-garden blossom thornless.

—ABŪ-SAʾID ABUL-KHAYR

OCTOBER 5

My God, may I cease to live the life of my own spirit so I might live in Your Divine life and in You alone: knowing through Your Light, loving through Your passion, and acting through Your power.

—JEAN-JACQUES OLIER

OCTOBER 6

O goodness! O Love! O extravagance of tenderness!
O God of passion and compassion! How can the hearts
of human beings be so frigid and frozen toward You,
who are ablaze with love for them? May all my joy and
delight be in thinking of You, in serving and loving
You! Oh my All, may all I am be totally Yours and may
You alone possess everything that belongs to me, that is
part of me and within me!

—John Eudes

OCTOBER 7

Here He is in my Heart: I believe,
help Thou my unbelief.
Adore Him, thank Him, and love Him for me:
He is your Son, His Honor is in Your hands.
Do not let me dishonor Him.

—DOROTHY DAY'S PRAYER TO MARY AFTER TAKING
COMMUNION

OCTOBER 8

Let me be one of those
Who does not care
For this world or for heaven—
Neither are of any concern
To the people of love
And the people of love
Are loved through their love.
Fire me with Your love
So I burn for You alone.

—ABU YAZID BISTAMI

OCTOBER 9

May I dare to love
As if there were only me and God
In the whole wide world.

—ANDREW HARVEY, INSPIRED BY BROTHER LAWRENCE OF
THE RESURRECTION

OCTOBER 10

Send me now, O God, any trial that You will:
I have means and power given to me by You
To acquit myself with honor through whatever happens.

—EPICTETUS

OCTOBER 11

Today, this once, my Beloved, don't go, accept
This frail tattered flower, this rose-on-fire
Take in, coquette, this sad-eyed shabby client
Embrace, flawless full moon, my boiling darkness.

—RUMI

OCTOBER 12

May what I do flow from me like a river.

—RAINIER MARIA RILKE

OCTOBER 13

In you is my joy
Even if you send me suffering
For, by your grace, I aspire
To be purified like gold in the fire.

—GREGORY NAZIANZUS

OCTOBER 14

Lord and Master of my life,
Take from me the spirit of laziness,
Discouragement, domination, and idle talk:
Grace to me, your servant,
A spirit of purity, humility, patience, love.
My lord and king, grant me to see my sins
And never to judge my neighbor
For you are blessed forever and ever.

—EPHREM THE SYRIAN

OCTOBER 15

Lord, lift the hard veil from my face
So before this weeping freezes again
I can set free a little of this despair
And misery that gorge on my heart.

—DANTE

OCTOBER 16

I pray to you, Lord
For the Holy gift of tears
So the hardness of my heart
Can be softened by being broken.

—EVAGRIUS OF PONTUS

OCTOBER 17

Sanctify me, O holy spirit, so that even when I am eating, drinking, or sleeping, the fragrance of prayer is spontaneously exhaled by my soul. Make my heart as boundlessly merciful as yours, embracing all beings and the world in a cosmic charity, a limitless hope even for the evil, even for the demons and the snakes. Transform me so utterly that all who come into my presence, human or animal, may know the mysterious Peace of your love.

—ANDREW HARVEY, INSPIRED BY ISAAC OF NINEVEH

OCTOBER 18

Teach us, Great Spirit,
To walk the soft earth
As relatives of all that live.

—LAKOTA PRAYER

OCTOBER 19

Lord, grace me through your holy spirit,
That, amid the tumult of outward cares
I should live inwardly in peace
In a calm reigning of love.

—GREGORY THE GREAT

OCTOBER 20

From the unreal lead me to the real!
From the darkness lead me to light!
From death lead me to immortality!

—Brihadaranyaka Upanishad

OCTOBER 21

My only safety; this shaky soaring
That skins all hope, all desire . . .
All I am is a bead on your string
Keep turning me with one finger.

—RUMI

OCTOBER 22

O Lord, calm the waves of this heart; calm its tempests!
Calm thyself, O my soul, so that the divine can act in
thee! Calm thyself, O my soul, so that God is able to
repose in thee, so that His peace may cover thee! Yes,
Father in Heaven, often have we found that the world
cannot give us peace, O but make us feel that Thou art
able to give peace; let us know the truth of Thy promise:
that the whole world may not be able to take away Thy
peace.

—SØREN KIERKEGAARD

OCTOBER 23

One who speaks ill of me is a hero for me;
He works without pay.
He is instrumental in enabling me
To wash off my old sins.
He renders me service without reward.
He sinks and saves others.
O Rama, I pray for his long life.
Dadu says, the vilifier is a benefactor in disguise.

—DADU DAYAL

October 24

The days go numb, the wind
Sucks the world from my senses
Like withered leaves.

Through the empty branches the sky remains.
It is what I have.
May I be Earth now, and even song.
May I be the ground under that sky.
May I be humble now, like a thing
Ripened until it is real
So that He who began it all
Can feel me when He reaches for me.

—ANDREW HARVEY, INSPIRED BY RAINER MARIA RILKE

OCTOBER 25

The Prophet Responds

Though the fig tree doesn't bloom,
and there's no produce
on the vine;
though the olive crop withers,
and the fields
don't provide food;
though the sheep is cut off
from the pen,
and there is no cattle
in the stalls;
I will rejoice in the Lord.

—HABAKKUK 3:17–18

OCTOBER 26

Lord, help me
See myself as I really am
And so be constantly rescued
From pride and vanity.
And help me to see You as You see me
And so know Your miraculous love
Constantly outspread to me
To rescue me from despair and self-pity.

—SUFI PRAYER

OCTOBER 27

Remember, O most gracious Virgin Mary, that never was it known that anyone who fled to your protection, implored your help, and sought your intercession was left unaided. Inspired by this confidence, I fly to you, O Virgin of Virgins, my Mother; to you I come, before you I stand sinful and sorrowful. O Mother of the Word Incarnate, despise not my petitions, but in thy mercy hear and answer me. Amen.

—BERNARD DE CLAIRVAUX

OCTOBER 28

Lord, save me from despair, and if I am
In despair, inspire me to reach out in compassion
To another, to do a work of peace for you.

—ALAN PATON

OCTOBER 29

Almighty and most merciful Father, we have erred and
strayed from thy ways like lost sheep. We have followed
too much the devices and desires of our own hearts.
We have offended against thy holy laws. We have left
undone those things we ought to have done and we have
done those things which we ought not to have done.

—ARCHBISHOP CRANMER OF CANTERBURY

OCTOBER 30

Lord
Grant me your oasis of prayer
And your garden of humble devotion
In the sandstorm of the vanishing world

—BEDOUIN PRAYER

OCTOBER 31

You made the fountain of brass flow for Solomon
And graced him power over all winds:
What I pray for is this one miracle—
That in all my darkest days and those of the world
I may always worship Your light.

—SUFI PRAYER BY ANDREW HARVEY

NOVEMBER

November 1

May I always know
The time of business is no different
From the time of prayer.
And in the noise and clatter of my kitchen
May I possess you as peacefully
As if I were on my knees
Before the Holy Sacrament.

—Andrew Harvey, inspired by Brother Lawrence of
the Resurrection

NOVEMBER 2

May the things not in my power be nothing to me.

—EPICTETUS

NOVEMBER 3

Give me, Beautiful Lord,
Insatiable longings for Your beauty.
For only such longings
Can constantly empty me of me
So You can fill me constantly
With ever-growing peace and bliss.
And birth Your splendor in me.

—RUMI

NOVEMBER 4

We have awakened and all of creation has awakened for God, Sustainer of all the worlds. God, I ask You for the best that day has to offer, opening, support, light, blessings, guidance, and I seek refuge in You from any harm in it and any harm that might come after it.

—THE PROPHET MUHAMMAD

November 5

Wherever I turn
May I see the Face of God.

—Sufi prayer by Andrew Harvey

November 6

Awake, O North wind,
And come, thou South: blow upon my garden
So its spices may flow out.

—Saint John of the Cross

November 7

O mover of miracles within me
Pour the healing waters of compassion
On the wounded body of humanity
And make it whole, make it whole!

—Ancient Sanskrit prayer

NOVEMBER 8

The Earth is beautiful
The Earth is beautiful
The Earth is beautiful
Below the East, the Earth, its face toward the East,
the top
Of its head is beautiful
Its legs, they are beautiful
Its body, it is beautiful
Its chest, it is beautiful
Its breath, it is beautiful
Its head feather, it is beautiful
The Earth is beautiful.

—Navajo song

NOVEMBER 9

Lion, symbol of the Kings of Zulu!
Lion, thunder of the valleys!
Where your roar is to be heard,
There life is found.
Where your breath is to be smelled,
Can walk no evil.
And where you are seen, there is no fear.
Lion, may your footprint never be erased
By the passing winds,
Long may you walk over the plains of the earth!

—AFRICAN SHAMANIC PRAYER

November 10

Should my body perish for the mission
You have entrusted to me.
Should it fall to the ground
And be trampled to fragments—
May your word and spirit be enough for me.
All the worst horrors happen only to the body—
May my love be yours, belong to you,
And remain with you forever, come what may.

—MARTIN LUTHER

November 11

Mother
Pillar of Fire
In this darkening desert
Help me follow you
Across the burning sands
Of my hopelessness and despair
To the country where your splendor reigns
And all the rocks and rivers chant your name.

—Romanus Melodus

NOVEMBER 12

Grant that whatever You want of me
I may give it to You freely
And that whatever You ask me to do
That it be done in me by You.

—SUFI PRAYER BY ANDREW HARVEY

November 13

O give me the grace to see Thy Face and be
A constant mirror of eternity.

—Thomas Traherne

NOVEMBER 14

Love has overcome.
Love is victorious.
Amen.

—SPONTANEOUS PRAYER OF THOMAS MERTON, A FEW DAYS
BEFORE HIS DEATH

NOVEMBER 15

Whatever way love's camel takes
May that be my religion, my faith.

—ANDREW HARVEY, INSPIRED BY IBN ARABI

November 16

Purge, O God, our minds of their horrible darknesses
And light Your eternal Light in our senses!

—Ancient alchemist's prayer

NOVEMBER 17

Give me that holy wild laughter
That laughs at death and defeat and desolation!
I have seen my devil and he is profound and grave.
And in his gravity life shipwrecks and drowns.
Let the God in me rise like a dancer, and laugh.

—Friedrich Nietzsche

November 18

We give you thanks, most gracious God, for the beauty of earth and sky and sea; for the richness of mountains, plains, and rivers; for the songs of birds and the loveliness of flowers. We praise you for these good gifts, and pray that we may safeguard them for our prosperity. Grant that we may continue to grow in our grateful enjoyment of your abundant creation, to the honor of your name, now and forever. Amen.

—The Book of Common Prayer

NOVEMBER 19

Ocean Spirit
Calm the waves for me.
Get close to me, my power
My heart is tired.
Make the sea milk for me.

—HAIDA SONG

November 20

Sever me from myself that I may be grateful to you;
May I perish to myself that I may be safe in you;
May I die to myself that I may live in you;
May I wither to myself that I may blossom in you;
May I be emptied to myself that I may abound in you;
May I be nothing to myself that I may be all to you.

—Desiderius Erasmus

November 21

Above all, Lord, give me the grace of compassion. Grant me to have compassion on sinners from the depth of my heart: for that is the supreme virtue. Grant me to have compassion every time I witness the fall of a sinner. Let me not arrogantly reprove him, but suffer and weep with him. And when I weep for my neighbor, may I weep for myself as well and apply to myself the words: the prostitute is more righteous than you are.

—AMBROSE, ARCHBISHOP OF MILAN

NOVEMBER 22

Lord, grant me to feel the power
Of the words that describe your mysteries.

—ISAAC OF NINEVEH

NOVEMBER 23

May I return evil with good
So my enemy may become my friend.

—SUFI PRAYER BY ANDREW HARVEY

November 24

My treasure and good fortune, Lord sweet as honey,
Golden flame of heaven, O form of blazing light,
My friend, my flesh,
Heart within my flesh, soul within my heart,
Wish-fulfilling tree,
My eye, dark pupil in the eye, image that dances within!
Save me from the hidden disease of karma.

—Appar "Hymn to Shiva"

November 25

The Roman Road: A Christian Speaks to a Lion in the Arena

Oh Lion in a peculiar guise,
Sharp Roman road to Paradise,
Come eat me up, I'll pay thy toll
With all my flesh, and keep my soul.

—Stevie Smith

November 26

My Lord God, I have no idea where I am going. I do
not see the road ahead of me. I cannot know for certain
where it will end. Nor do I really know myself, and the
fact that I think I am following your will does not mean
that I am actually doing so. But I believe that the desire
to please you does in fact please you. And I hope I have
that desire in all that I am doing. I hope that I will never
do anything apart from that desire. And I know that if
I do this, you will lead me by the right road, though I
may know nothing about it. Therefore I will trust you
always though I may seem to be lost and in the shadow
of death. I will not fear, for you are ever with me, and
you will never leave me to face my perils alone.

—Thomas Merton

NOVEMBER 27

Those You give robes of honor
Are distracted from You by their robes.
May I never wish anything from You
Other than You.

—ABU YAZID BISTAMI

November 28

Prayer to Isis

My call is to Isis,
she of the shining spirit.

Isis, come among us,
we who enter the timeless
together.

Oh, Isis,
let me be your creature,
to serve you

Let me sleep
beneath your breast,
where energy flows.

Isis, let your voice
come into my throat,
your presence
unwind the dance
in its slow spiral.

—Dorothy Walters

November 29

The truth in you remains
as radiant as a star,
as pure as light,
as innocent as love itself.

—*A Course in Miracles*

NOVEMBER 30

I'm poured out like water.
All my bones have fallen apart.
My heart is like wax;
it melts inside me.
My strength is dried up
like a piece of broken pottery.
My tongue sticks
to the roof of my mouth;
you've set me down
in the dirt of death.
Dogs surround me;
a pack of evil people circle me
like a lion—
oh, my poor hands and feet!
I can count all my bones!
Meanwhile, they just stare at me,
watching me.
They divvy up my garments
among themselves;
they cast lots for my clothes.

But you, Lord! Don't be far away!
You are my strength!
Come quick and help me!
Deliver me from the sword.
Deliver my life from the power
of the dog.

—PSALM 22:14–20

DECEMBER

DECEMBER 1

Marry within me, O Beloved
Your peace and your great holy wildness
The deepest calm of contemplation
With the molten courage to risk everything
To put your divine will into action.

—ANDREW HARVEY

DECEMBER 2

Let what is necessary to be taken away
Be taken away
Let what is necessary to be given
Be given
I know nothing of either
But I know You do
And I surrender to You
To do to me whatever Your Love wants to.

—CAROLINE MYSS

DECEMBER 3

Incline us O God! To think humbly of ourselves . . .
to consider our fellow-creatures with kindness, and to
judge of all they say and do with the charity which we
would desire from them ourselves.

—JANE AUSTEN

DECEMBER 4

O Lord, I beg You for good health in this world and safety in the hereafter. O Lord, I beg you for Your mercy and benevolence in the affairs of my life and my religion, in what I own, for myself and my household. Make us safe from the things we fear and hide our faults. O Lord, I take refuge in You from evil coming from before me and behind me, from my left and right, and from above. Protect me from what may come from below to destroy me.

—The Prophet Muhammad

December 5

Let me go on drinking
Cup after cup of love.
Let the wine never run out.
Let my thirst never be satisfied.

—Abd al-Karīm ibn Hawāzin al-Qushayri

DECEMBER 6

Gracious God, the comfort of all who sorrow, the strength of all who suffer: Let the cry of those in misery and need come to you, that they may find your mercy present with them in all their afflictions; and give us, we pray, the strength to serve them for the sake of him who suffered for us, your Son Jesus Christ our Lord. Amen.

—THE BOOK OF COMMON PRAYER

DECEMBER 7

May I know, through Your grace,
That both of us are a single worshipper
Who, through the grace of unity,
Bows Himself to His own essence
In every act of bowing—
For no one prays to You but You
And no one prays to anyone but the You in them.

—IBN FARID

December 8

Lord,
If you have blessings to give me,
Give them to those who do not know Your mercy.
And to those who have brought on themselves misery,
Let the peace You have given me be theirs.
And to those who wander in arrogant darkness,
As I have wandered before you called me,
Grant that their hearts may come to bow to you
On this plain and threadbare mat of tears.

—SUFI PRAYER BY ANDREW HARVEY

DECEMBER 9

May it not be Your gifts I look for Lord
But Yourself, so I can be content with nothing less.

—BROTHER LAWRENCE OF THE RESURRECTION

December 10

I cry out to you
because you answer me.
So tilt your ears toward me now—
listen to what I am saying!
Manifest your faithful love
in amazing ways
because you are the one
who saves those
who take refuge in you,
saving them from their attackers
by your strong hand.
Watch me with the very pupil
of your eye!
Hide me in the protection
of your wings.

—PSALM 17:6—8

DECEMBER 11

Zarathustra's Prayer

Let my animals guide me!
For I have found it
More dangerous
Among men than among animals.

—Friedrich Nietzsche

DECEMBER 12

O Mother of all grace, all beauty,
You are the paradise of God.
From you springs the fountain of living
water that irrigates all the universe.
I stand before you, your child: fill me with You.

—BERNARD DE CLAIRVAUX

DECEMBER 13

More honorable than the seraphim
More incomparably glorious than the cherubim
How, Mother, can any human mind know
How to praise you fittingly?
Help me, illumine me, live in me
Make me the servant of your infinite compassion
Make all my actions radiate your healing grace.

—ANDREW HARVEY IN THE ORTHODOX TRADITION

DECEMBER 14

With clasped hands I entreat the perfectly
Enlightened Ones who stand in all the regions,
That they kindle the lamp of the Law for them
Who in their blindness fall into sorrow.

—SHANTIDEVA

DECEMBER 15

May I realize truth, and become one with truth!
May I, through vision of the divine, become divine!

—SRI RAMAKRISHNA

DECEMBER 16

All the harm with which the world is rife
All fear and suffering that exist
Clings to the "I" that caused it—
May wisdom exorcise this great demon!

—TIBETAN PRAYER

DECEMBER 17

O Fire,
May you be endured by us
With noble gratitude
So you become
The supreme blossoming
And expansion of our whole being.

—THE RIG VEDA

December 18

We do not know what is best
Nor for what we should pray.
You know, great God. Give it to us!

—Khond tribe of Orissa

DECEMBER 19

May I always, both through prayer and action,
Pay homage to You, Tara, the Mother,
Who protects the entire world
From the eight terrors
Who saves us all from poverty and danger
May I and all sentient beings
Live awake in Your all-healing presence
And grow enlightened through Your saving compassion.

—ANDREW HARVEY IN THE TIBETAN TRADITION

DECEMBER 20

"O Moon, folded in my sweet embrace,
Be you as strong as I, as fair of face."
"O Sun, brightest of all lights known to men,
May you desire me, as the cock the hen."

—ALCHEMIST PRAYER OF SACRED MARRIAGE

DECEMBER 21

Love is sweeter than life
Sweeter than honey and the honeycomb
And does not shirk from any agony
For those it loves.
Love is the golden child of knowledge.
Lord, fill me with eternal love.

—ISAAC OF NINEVEH

December 22

Save us in the deep!
Save us from the storm!
Bring us to land safe!

—Ancient Melanesian folk song

DECEMBER 23

O heavenly Father, who hast filled the world with beauty: open our eyes to behold thy gracious hand in all thy works; that, rejoicing in thy whole creation, we may learn to serve thee with gladness; for the sake of him through whom all things were made, thy Son Jesus Christ our Lord. Amen.

—THE BOOK OF COMMON PRAYER

DECEMBER 24

May the humility of the Cross
Always be more beautiful to me
Than all the glories of the world.

—BROTHER LAWRENCE OF THE RESURRECTION

DECEMBER 25

I reverently speak in the presence of the Great Parent God: I pray that this day, the whole day, as a child of God, I may not be taken hold of by my own desire, but show forth the divine glory by living a life of creativity, which shows forth the true individual.

—MORNING SHINTO PRAYER

DECEMBER 26

Lord
Send down upon me
The spirit of serenity
So all my thoughts and actions
Can breathe the grace of Your peace.

—SUFI PRAYER BY ANDREW HARVEY

December 27

Almighty God, king of heaven and earth,
I give you thanks for the gift of the law
By which I can impress on my flesh my love for you.

—Jewish prayer

December 28

Oh you Gods,
take this life and use it.

Take this body
and strengthen it.

Take this heart
and open it.

Take all of me and, oh
you Gods, do not waste a drop!

—Janine Canan

DECEMBER 29

O Virgin
Who abandoned Your soul in Joy
By offering it to God
Grant that in our gift to God
Our joy may be complete
And be for us the foundation
In which it can always be renewed.

—SAINT MACARIUS

DECEMBER 30

I proclaim myself homeless in time.
I proclaim myself homeless in space.
I proclaim myself homeless in the heavens.
I proclaim myself homeless in all things
Except in God, eternal, infinite, and silent.
Burn me, O Fire, until I am no more.

—SRI RAMAKRISHNA

December 31

Holy Mary
Star of the sea
Guide me safely over
The dark tragic waters
Of your world in transformation.

—Andrew Harvey

PERMISSIONS

Paul Ballanfat, "May He Grant Us the Grace of His Beauty," excerpt from *The Nightingale in the Garden of Love* (Anqa Publishing, 2005).

Janine Canan, "You are Playing Your Music Again," May I be Your Riverbed," "Oh You Gods," and "This is Your Body, Mother" poems by Janine Canan from *Ardor: Poems of Life* (Pilgrims, Varanasi, 2012; available in USA from JanineCanan.com).

Cesar Chavez, "Prayer of the Farm Workers' Struggle," TM/© 2013 the Cesar Chavez Foundation www.chaves foundation.org.

"Strengthen Us O God" by Oliver Cromwell, taken from *Seasons of Devotion* by Philip Law, Continuum, an imprint of Bloomsbury Plc.

Lex Hixon, "I Would Not Even Care to Be an Emperor" excerpt from *Mother of the Universe,* ©1994 This Material was reproduced by permission of Quest Books, the imprint of The Theosophical Publishing House (www.questbooks.net).

Francis Jammes, "Prayer to Be Simple," "Prayer to Confess One's Ignorance," "Oh My Guardian Angel," and "Prayer to Praise God" excerpts from *Under the Azure: Poems of Francis Jammes,* translated by Janine Canan (Littlefox Press, Melbourne, 2010).

"The Road Ahead" from *Thoughts in Solitude* by Thomas Merton. Copyright © 1958 by the Abbey of Our Lady of Gethsemani. Copyright renewed 1986 by the Trustees of the Thomas Merton Legacy Trust. Reprinted by permission of Farrar, Straus and Giroux, LLC.

"Let Me Be Silent" and "Let What Is Necessary to Be Taken Away," by Caroline Myss used by permission of the author.

"O God, a Child is Crying," "Let Me Accept the Defeats that have Adorned my Journey," "Remind Us O God, of Your Dream," "May We Become the Longing of our Ancestors," and "Unchain my Soul O Lord," by Chris Saade. © 2013 Chris Saade. Used with permission.

ACKNOWLEDGMENTS

To Nancy Steinbeck, beloved conspirator.

To Michael and Miles Steinbeck, beloved buddies.

To Frances Cohoon, Druid guide and oracle.

To Anne Lynne Andrews, rock and safe harbor.

To Michael Cohoon, unfailing friend.

To Eric Warner, beloved brother.

To Charlene and Tony Marshall, witnesses of Christ.

To Patricia Gift, old friend and peerless editor.

To Quressa Robinson, for her wonderful wise precision.

To Ned Leavitt, my ever patient agent.

To Sheryl Leach, without whom . . . nothing.

To Janet Thomas, for all her courage.

To Gloria Vanderbilt, for all her enduring love.

To Diane Berke, whose life is a prayer.

To Laura Gray, for her ultimate precision.

ABOUT THE
AUTHOR

Andrew Harvey is an internationally acclaimed poet, novelist, translator, mystical scholar, and spiritual teacher. He was born in South India in 1952, moved to England at age nine, and later attended Oxford University, where in 1973 he became a Fellow of All Souls College. In 1977, he returned to India for the first time since his childhood and underwent several mystical experiences, which began a series of initiations into different mystical traditions to learn their secrets and practices.

Harvey has taught at Oxford University, Cornell University, Hobart and William Smith Colleges, The California Institute of Integral Studies, and the University of Creation Spirituality (now Wisdom University), as well as at various churches and spiritual centers throughout the United States, England, and Europe. He is the author of more than 30 books, including *The Hope, Son of Man, The Direct Path, Hidden Journey, The Essential Mystics, The Way of Passion: A Celebration of Rumi, The Return of the Mother, A Journey in Ladakh, Sun at Midnight: A Memoir of the Dark Night,* and his most recent work, *Radical Passion.*

Harvey was the subject of the 1993 BBC documentary *The Making of a Modern Mystic* and has appeared in several others, including *Rumi Turning Ecstatic, The Return of Rumi, The Consciousness of the Christ, In the Fire of Grace,* and a documentary on the life and work of Marion Woodman. His own 90-minute documentary *Sacred Activism* was produced by the Hartley Film Foundation in 2005.

He is the founder and director of the Institute of Sacred Activism and lives in a log cabin in Arkansas.

NOTES

NOTES

NOTES

NOTES

Hay House Titles of Related Interest

YOU CAN HEAL YOUR LIFE, the movie,
starring Louise L. Hay & Friends
(available as a 1-DVD program and an expanded 2-DVD set)
Watch the trailer at: **www.LouiseHayMovie.com**

THE SHIFT, the movie,
starring Dr. Wayne W. Dyer
(available as a 1-DVD program and an expanded 2-DVD set)
Watch the trailer at: **www.DyerMovie.com**

ବଦଡ଼

SAVED BY A POEM: The Transformative Power of Words,
Kim Rosen

*FOR LOVERS OF GOD EVERYWHERE: Poems of the Christian
Mystics,* by Roger Housden

REVEAL: A Sacred Manual for Getting Spiritually Naked,
by Meggan Watterson

All of the above are available at your local bookstore,
or may be ordered by contacting Hay House (see next page).

ବଦଡ଼

We hope you enjoyed this Hay House book. If you'd like to receive our online catalog featuring additional information on Hay House books and products, or if you'd like to find out more about the Hay Foundation, please contact:

Hay House, Inc., P.O. Box 5100, Carlsbad, CA 92018-5100
(760) 431-7695 or (800) 654-5126
(760) 431-6948 (fax) or (800) 650-5115 (fax)
www.hayhouse.com® • **www.hayfoundation.org**

ର୧ ৩

Published and distributed in Australia by: Hay House Australia Pty. Ltd., 18/36 Ralph St., Alexandria NSW 2015 • *Phone:* 612-9669-4299 • *Fax:* 612-9669-4144 • www.hayhouse.com.au

Published and distributed in the United Kingdom by: Hay House UK, Ltd., Astley House, 33 Notting Hill Gate, London W11 3JQ • *Phone:* 44-20-3675-2450 • *Fax:* 44-20-3675-2451 • www.hayhouse.co.uk

Published and distributed in the Republic of South Africa by: Hay House SA (Pty), Ltd., P.O. Box 990, Witkoppen 2068 • *Phone/Fax:* 27-11-467-8904 • www.hayhouse.co.za

Published in India by: Hay House Publishers India, Muskaan Complex, Plot No. 3, B-2, Vasant Kunj, New Delhi 110 070 • *Phone:* 91-11-4176-1620 • *Fax:* 91-11-4176-1630 • www.hayhouse.co.in

Distributed in Canada by: Raincoast, 9050 Shaughnessy St., Vancouver, B.C. V6P 6E5 • *Phone:* (604) 323-7100 • *Fax:* (604) 323-2600 • www.raincoast.com

ର୧ ৩

Take Your Soul on a Vacation

Visit **www.HealYourLife.com®** to regroup, recharge, and reconnect with your own magnificence.
Featuring blogs, mind-body-spirit news, and life-changing wisdom from Louise Hay and friends.

Visit **www.HealYourLife.com** today!